The Ancient Wisdom of the Chinese
Their Philosophy in Sayings and Proverbs

Edited with an Introduction By Brian Brown
And a Preface by Ly Hoi Sang

Published by Soul Care Publishing

CONTENTS

PREFACE 1
INTRODUCTION 3
CONFUCIUS. 551 B.C. - ANALECTS 7
ON GOVERNING 7
TRUE GOODNESS 7
THE PRINCELY MAN 8
ON PRETENSE 8
EXALTED VIRTUE 8
ON BEING DISTINGUISHED 8
NOBLE CHARACTER 9
POWER OF EXAMPLE 10
THE NINE POINTS 10
THE FIVE QUALITIES 10
RIGHTEOUSNESS 10
ON HATE 11
THE FOUR WORDS 11
CONFUCIUS ON HIMSELF 11
ON OBSERVATION 13
PROMINENCE 13
SELF-CONTROL 14
MEDITATION 14
LIFE AND DEATH 14
RICH AND POOR 15
VIRTUE FOR EFFECT 15
ON TEACHING 15
SHADOWS AND VIRTUES 16
DOES GOD SPEAK 16

SERVANTS 16
TRUE VALUES 17
SAYINGS OF THE DISCIPLES 17
CONFUCIUS - THE DOCTRINE OF THE MEAN 18
ON TRUTH 18
REALIZATION OF TRUTH 18
ABSOLUTE TRUTH 19
TRUTH AND INTELLIGENCE 19
TRUTH AND THE COSMIC LAWS 20
TRUTH AND KNOWLEDGE 20
TRUTH AND FOREKNOWLEDGE 20
MORAL LAW 21
FORCE OF CHARACTER 22
HOLDING TO THE MORAL LAW 22
UNDERSTANDING THE MORAL LAW 22
THE UNIVERSE AND THE MORAL MIND 23
PRACTICE OF THE MORAL LAW 23
FOUR POINTS OF THE MORAL LAW 24
IMPROVEMENT 24
SELF-CONTROL UNDER ALL CIRCUMSTANCES 24
SELF-ANALYSIS 25
BEGINNING AT THE BOTTOM 25
MORAL LAW AND NATURE 26
GIFTS OF THE MORALLY PERFECT 26
SPIRITUAL FORCES 27
KNOWLEDGE OF MORALS 28
PERSONAL CONDUCT 29
THE FOOLISH 29
LIFE OF THE MORAL MAN 29

CONFUCIUS - THE GREAT LEARNING 31
THE TRUE SCHOLAR 31
MENCIUS. 371 B.C. - THE REAL MAN 33
THE WARNING VOICE WITHIN 33
THE DISCIPLINE OF HEAVEN 34
CONCERNING DESIRES 34
THE CHILD-HEART 34
EQUANIMITY 35
THE END OF WISDOM IS TO SEEK THE LOST MIND 35
GREATNESS 35
THE WISE 37
THE TRUE AND THE FALSE 37
TRANSCENDENTALISM 38
QUALITIES OF THE GREAT 38
APPOINTMENTS OF THE GREAT 38
RESPONSIBILITIES OF THE GOVERNMENT 39
LAO TZU. 604 B.C. - FROM THE TAO-TEH KING 44
THE SPIRITUAL AND MATERIAL 45
THE FORM OF TAO 45
THE FORCE OF TAO 45
THE INFINITE 46
THE GREATNESS OF TAO 46
THE UNCHANGING TAO 47
HIGHEST AND LOWEST 47
NATURAL LAW AND TAO 47
THE FIRST CAUSE 48
THE WAY OF HEAVEN 48
ON SELF-ASSERTION 48

ON PERFECT VIRTUE 49
THE SUPERIOR SCHOLAR 49
DISPLAY 49
BEGIN HARMONY WITH YOUR AGE 50
MODERATION IN GOVERNMENT 50
ANCIENT PHILOSOPHERS 50
ON THE NATURE OF THINGS 51
LAO TZU - WU-WEI 54
ON SELF-DISPLAY 55
ON RULING THE PEOPLE 57
LAO TZU - PRECEPTS AND SAYINGS 59
CHUANG TZU. 400 B. C - . RIGHT AND WRONG 66
THE TRUE STANDARD 66
ON CONSCIOUSNESS 66
KNOWLEDGE AND ATTAINMENT 67
THE NATURAL ORDER 67
THE SOUL 68
OBJECTIVE AND SUBJECTIVE 68
ON LIFE AND DEATH 68
INFINITE 69
FINALITY 70
NATURAL INSTINCTS 71
SEVERANCE 72
YANG CHU. 300 B.C. - FAME AND VANITY 74
THE FOUR CHIMERAS 76
KANG-HSI'S SACRED EDICT 78
KUAN-YI-WU. 500 B.C. – ON LIFE 81
YU TSE. 1250 B.C. – ON FAME 82
TSE-CHAN. 550 B.C. 83

SUBLIMITY OF RIGHTEOUSNESS 83
THE POETRY OF THE CHINESE 84
SSU-K'UNG T'U, A.D. 834-908 84
CH'ANG CH'IEN. A.D. 720 85
TS'EN-TS'AN. A.D. 750 85
PO CHU-I. A.D. 772 86
MYSELF 86
LAO TZU 87
OU-YANG HSIU. A.D. 1007 87
ANON. 87
ANON 88
ANON. A.D. 1715 88
CHIA I. 200 B.C. - CALLED THE POE OF CHINA 89
SU WU 90
PAN CHIH YU. 18 B.C. - THE SAPPHO OF CHINA 91
ANON. 92
LI PO - THE POPE OF HIS AGE 92
PROVERBS AND MAXIMS 94
ABSENT-MINDEDNESS 94
ACCURACY 94
BUSINESS 94
COMPENSATIONS 94
DIFFICULTIES 94
DIVINE PROVIDENCE 95
EDUCATION 95
FAMILY 95
GAMBLING 95
FRIENDSHIP 95

GOVERNMENT 95
GRATITUDE 96
HEEDLESSNESS 96
HONESTY 96
HUMANITY 96
HUSBANDS AND WIVES 97
HUMILITY 97
INDUSTRY 97
INSTINCT 97
KNOWLEDGE 97
LAWSUITS 98
VANITY OF LIFE 98
MAN 98
OPPORTUNITY 98
PHYSICIANS 98
PROCRASTINATION 99
PRACTICAL RELIGION 99
SELF-CONTROL 99
YOUTH 99
WINE 99
WOMAN 99
SERVICE 100
SKILL 100
VIRTUE 100
GENERAL 100
MORAL MAXIMS 101
BIBLIOGRAPHY AND SOURCES 116

PREFACE

We say, in China: "Confucius! Confucius'! How great Confucius! Before Confucius there never was a Confucius. Since Confucius there never has been a Confucius. How great is Confucius!"

In the Western world someone has said: "Confucius invented wisdom," and when you find sayings of his like this one — "When you know a thing, to hold that you know it, and when you do not, to admit the fact, — this is knowledge," you are willing to allow him the title.

Confucius and his greatest follower Mencius were reformers in the true sense of the word. Their whole aim was to construct personal character, and they demanded that the moral and spiritual nature should be substituted for the might of the strong.

No rank was too high, no class too humble, to be taught this universal principle; and with no other personal authority than their own honest conviction, these men went forth to demand of kings and peoples the square acceptance of its claims.

When Confucius was thirty-three years of age he visited Lao Tzu, who was then eighty- seven; and it is recorded that the great founder of Taoism was not much impressed by the younger man.

Lao Tzu was a mystic; his Wu Wei means "do nothing," the supposed meaning of which is: get in harmony with the great Spirit of things and you will be unconsciously impelled to right action — in other words, do nothing with self- will. Confucius, on the other hand, was a practical man, a teacher of ethics, who thought by self-conscious direction one could arrive at proper action. To Lao Tzu, Confucius seemed a materialist, so it is not strange that the young man did not impress the older one.

Both these great men, though they differ in method, are the substance of the Chinese consciousness, the race-mold or type; they have left their mark upon their people. They were illumined men, lighted with the spirit to see and do right. They had the power to make clear the path for others; they went about introducing the noble thoughts that lead to the higher life, and they inspired true confidence by practicing what they preached.

Both sages inspired great followers; the great exponent of Confucius was Mencius, who proved himself worthy of his master; the great exponent of the doctrines of Lao Tzu was Chuang Tzu, himself a mystic, and by nature fitted for the interpretation of the mystical teachings of the Tao which could be translated as "Way," — meaning the spiritual "Way" or path trodden by those having a close contact with nature. Lao Tzu said: "Go back to Mother Nature, for lying on her bosom, you will be guided on the proper way."

I hope that this book of wise sayings, selected and collected by Mr. Brown, will be the power for showing some people in the Western world the way back to Mother Nature and her Tao.

I am sure that the great American people, broad-minded and fair, are only too willing to investigate and give value to the thoughts of my people.

LY HOI SANG
Author of "A Collection of Pearls."

INTRODUCTION

Sir Robert Hart in his book, "The Eastern Question," says of the Chinese: "They are well-behaved, law-abiding, intelligent, economical, and industrious; they can learn anything and do anything; they are punctiliously polite; they worship talent, and they believe in right so firmly that they scorn to think it requires to be supported or enforced by might; they delight in literature, and everywhere they have their little clubs and coteries for learning and discussing each others' essays and verses; they possess and practice an admirable system of ethics, and they are generous, charitable, and fond of good works; they never forget a favor, they make rich return for any kindness, and though they know that money will buy service, a man must be more than wealthy to gain public esteem and respect; they are practical, teachable, and wonderfully gifted with common sense; they are excellent artisans, reliable workmen, and of a good faith that everyone acknowledges and admires in their commercial dealings; in no country has 'Honor thy father and mother' been so religiously obeyed, or so fully, and without exception given effect to, and this is in fact the keynote of their family, social,, official, and national life, and because it is so their days are long in the land God has given them."

It is very strange, when you consider the above tribute, and when, upon delving into the history of the Chinese — their arts, literature, and philosophy — you find that they had produced their greatest literature when Hammurabi was making laws for young Babylon; or before the city of Rome had been founded; and that they had great thinkers before Socrates or Plato appeared in Greece: yet if you will look in the histories of philosophies published in the West you will not find one mention of the Chinese thinkers.

It may be that the Western mind, the academic one in mean, is repelled by the form in which the Chinese sages used to express their thoughts. The philosophy of the Chinese is expressed for the most part by short sayings, proverbs, and maxims, brought out in conversation with their disciples, in the manner of Socrates and his disciples. This, to the Western mind, does not seem so interesting as to begin with a method — a system of philosophy, in fact, beginning with a well- defined idea, and finishing with what is called a logical conclusion.

The Chinese philosophy is called "not complete" because of this lack of Developed Methods, logic — observation — induction and deduction. What philosophy is complete? Is life complete? Has the whole sum of human experience been exhausted, and can man experience no more? Is the evolution of human consciousness at an end? The mind of man is not made; it is in the making. Every day something is added to our consciousness that was not there before. Truth is being revealed by a slow growth of consciousness, not by prophecy.

Prophecy offers to answer for evolution and all collectivism sooner or later becomes absolutism. Most methods of philosophy have absolutism and prophecy at their base — religions are an example of this; philosophy should be free from academic methods; so also should the arts be free in their expression. The Great Spirit never gave an individual an inspiration that at the same time he did not give the symbol of expression with it.

This is an, age in which technique is overdeveloped; in fact it has almost taken the place of inspiration. Conscious creation through the will is the order of the day, and every other person you meet is a "self-willed genius." Pictures are painted with method, but no soul; poetry is written, but the only inspiration in it is a new idea of how to construct in language: as though the symbol and not the idea is poetic.

Books of philosophical essays are written, following some method of reasoning, containing myriads of words and mountains of confusion, but not one new idea. Here again method seems to be taking the place of inspiration. To have common sense in your day is to be a philosopher. Socrates said, "Do not call me wise — I am not a wise man, I am only a searcher after wisdom."

Confucius said the same thing many years before: "Be not self-deceived in wisdom, look farther." Lao Tzu, B.C. 604, the Chinese mystic, would correspond to the early Christian mystics; he came to spiritual understanding through the higher spiritual emotion and not through intellect. Professor Gobelenz said of Lao Tzu's great work, the "Tao Teh King": "One of the most eminent masterpieces of the Chinese language; one of the profoundest books of philosophy the world has ever produced."

The Chinese language is admirably adapted to the epigrams and proverbs expressed in this beautiful work; his mysticism is hard to penetrate, but is filled with the most valuable spiritual guidance. As he himself says, "Only one who is eternally free from passions can comprehend its spiritual essence."

Confucius was a great moral teacher; he was more interested in the social structure than Lao Tzu. He taught that virtue and high moral conduct are developed through behavior; Lao Tzu — that the spiritual is everything. Confucius said, "Do not do to others what you would not have them do to you." His idea of love was not sentimental, it was more practical; he was a practical idealist. He said, "Do justice to thy neighbor."

His whole system is based on nothing more than understanding human nature and perfecting the individual through moral education. To him the attainment of perfect virtue was the true aim of living. His moral philosophical sayings are worthy to stand alongside of the Greek, Latin, or Hebrew teachers.

He deserves to be mentioned with Moses, for he dedicated his life to the improvement of his fellow-man. He set forth seven rules necessary for improvement. They are: The investigation of things; the completion of knowledge; the sincerity of thoughts and acts; the rectifying of the heart; the cultivation of the person; the regulation of the family and the government. Mencius, B.C. 372, was first a Taoist, but later on he became the most brilliant exponent of Confucius. He advocated many radical measures of reform,— universal education, free trade, and that only land should be taxed, as in Henry George's "Single Tax Theory."

Mencius said: "I love life, and I love righteousness. If I cannot have both, I choose righteousness." He also could be mentioned with the world's greatest thinkers.

Chuang Tzu was the greatest propagandist of Taoism. He might correctly be called the "Tao- saturated Man," as Spinoza was called the "God-intoxicated Man." He protested against the artificiality and materialism of his day and advocated a return to nature.

Yang Chu, the Epicurean of China, was the very opposite to Confucius, Lao-Tzu, and their followers, in his philosophy. He evolved a philosophy for life in which all is centered in the senses, and taught that the cultivation of the senses is the true basis of philosophy.

The other sages, included in this very incomplete anthology, are represented by what appears to be their most prominent expression. Their philosophy explains itself; their ideas are about life and things, the same as our own. Their race consciousness is very old and their views of life and things are mellowed by long experience.

Through a long contact and complete intimacy with nature, a philosophy of life was imparted to them. They unconsciously gave expression to the inward feelings and emotions that the cosmic law — the all divine — functioning in the material, imparted to them.

Their thought added to our Western thought should result in an eclecticism of great value to us both.

CONFUCIUS. 551 B.C. - ANALECTS

ON GOVERNING.

Chi K'ang Tzu questioned Confucius on a point of government, saying: "Ought not I to cut off the lawless in order to establish law and order? What do you think? " — Confucius replied: "Sir, what need is there of the death penalty in your system of government? If you showed a sincere desire to be good, your people would likewise be good. The virtue of the prince is like unto wind; that of the people, like unto grass. For it is the nature of grass to bend, when the wind blows upon it."

TRUE GOODNESS

Yen Yuan inquired as to the meaning of true goodness. The Master said: "The subdual of self, and reversion to the natural laws governing conduct— this is true goodness. If a man can for the space of one day subdue his selfishness and revert to natural laws, the whole world will call him good. True goodness springs from a man's own heart. How can it depend on other men?" — Yen Yuan said: "Kindly tell me the practical rule to be deduced from this." — The Master replied: "Do not use your eyes, your ears, your power of speech or your faculty of movement without obeying the inner law of self-control." — Yen Yuan said: "Though I am not quick in thought or act, I will make it my business to carry out this precept."

THE PRINCELY MAN

Ssu-Ma Niu asked for a definition of the princely man. The Master said: "The princely man is one who knows neither grief nor fear."— Absence of grief and fear! Is it the mark of a princely man? — The Master said: "If on searching his heart he finds no guilt, why should he grieve? of what should he be afraid?"

ON PRETENSE

It has not been my lot to see a divine man; could I see a princely man, that would satisfy me. It has not been my lot to see a thoroughly virtuous man; could I see a man possessing honesty of soul, that would satisfy me. Is it possible there should be honesty of soul in one who pretends to have what he has not; who, when empty, pretends to be overflowing; who, when in want, pretends to be in affluence?

EXALTED VIRTUE

Tzu Chang asked how to attain exalted virtue. The Master said: "Make conscientiousness and truth your guiding principles, and thus pass on to the cultivation of duty to your neighbor. This is exalted virtue."

ON BEING DISTINGUISHED

Tzu Chang asked: "What must a man do in order to be considered distinguished?" —The Master said: "What do you mean by the term distinguished?" — Tzu Chang replied: "I mean one whose fame fills both his own private circle and the State at large." — The Master said: "That is notoriety, not distinction. The man of true distinction is simple, honest, and a lover of justice and duty. He weighs men's words, and observes the expression of their faces.

"He is anxious to put himself below others. Such a one is truly distinguished in his private and his public life. As to the man who is merely much talked about, he puts on an appearance of charity and benevolence, but his actions belie it. He is self-satisfied and has no misgivings.

"Neither in private nor in public life does he achieve more than notoriety."

NOBLE CHARACTER

The Master said: "The higher type of man makes a sense of duty the groundwork of his character, blends with it in action a sense of harmonious proportion, manifests it in a sense of unselfishness, and perfects it by the addition of sincerity and truth. Then indeed is he a noble character."

The higher type of man seeks all that he wants in himself; the inferior man seeks all that he wants from others.

The higher type of man is firm but not quarrelsome; sociable, but not clannish.

The wise man does not esteem a person more highly because of what he says, neither does he undervalue what is said because of the person who says it.

Is not he a sage who neither anticipates deceit nor suspects bad faith in others, yet is prompt to detect them when they appear?

POWER OF EXAMPLE

Master wished to settle among the nine Eastern tribes. Someone said: "How can you? They are savages." The Master replied: "If a higher type of men dwelt in their midst, how could their savage condition last?"

THE NINE POINTS

The noble sort of man pays special attention to nine points. He is anxious to see clearly, to hear distinctly, to be kindly in his looks, respectful in his demeanor, conscientious in his speech, earnest in his affairs; when in doubt, he is careful to inquire; when in anger, he thinks of the consequences; when offered an opportunity for gain, he thinks only of his duty.

THE FIVE QUALITIES

Tzu Chang asked Confucius a question about Moral virtue. Confucius replied, "Moral virtue simply consists in being able, anywhere and everywhere, to exercise five particular qualities." Asked what these were, he said: "Self-respect, magnanimity, sincerity, earnestness, and benevolence. Show self-respect, and others will respect you; be magnanimous, and you will win all hearts; be sincere, and men will trust you; be earnest, and you will achieve great things; be benevolent, and you will be fit to impose your will on others."

RIGHTEOUSNESS

Tzu Lu asked: "Does not the princely man value courage?" The Master said: "He puts righteousness first.

The man of high station who has courage without righteousness is a menace to the State; the common man who has courage without righteousness is nothing more than a brigand."

ON HATE

Tzu Kung asked: "Has the nobler sort of man any hatreds?" The Master replied: "He has. He .hates those who publish the faults of others; he hates men of low condition who vilify those above them; he hates those whose courage is unaccompanied by self-restraint; he hates those who are audacious but narrow-minded."

"And you, Tzu," he added, "have you also your hatreds?" "I hate," replied the disciple, "those who think that wisdom consists in prying and meddling; courage, in showing no compliance; and honesty, in denouncing other men."

THE FOUR WORDS

There were four words of which the Master barred the use: He would have no "shall's," no "must's," certainly no "I's."

CONFUCIUS ON HIMSELF

At fifteen, my mind was bent on learning. At thirty I stood firm. At forty I was free from dclusions. At fifty I understood the laws of Providence. At sixty my ears were attentive to the truth. At seventy I could follow the promptings of my heart without overstepping the mean.

The failure to cultivate virtue, the failure to examine and analyze what I have learnt, the inability to move toward righteousness after being shown the way, the inability to correct my faults — these are the causes of my grief.

I do not expound my teaching to any who are not eager to learn; I do not help out anyone who is not anxious to explain himself; if, after being shown one corner of a subject, a man cannot go on to discover the other three, I do not repeat the lesson.

If the pursuit of riches were a commendable pursuit, I would join in it, even if I had to become a chariot-driver for the purpose. But seeing that it is not a commendable pursuit, I engage in those which are more to my taste.

The Master said: "In me, knowledge is not innate. I am but one who loves antiquity and is earnest in the study of it."

If I am walking with two other men, each of them will serve as my teacher. I will pick out the good points of one and imitate them, and the bad points of the other and correct them in myself.

There are men, I dare say, who act rightly without knowing the reason why, but I am not one of them. Having heard much, I sift out the good and practice it; having seen much, I retain it in my memory. This is the second order of wisdom.

To divide wisdom and perfect virtue I can lay no claim. All that can be said of me is that I never falter in the course which I pursue and am unwearying in my instruction of others — this and nothing more.] Kung-hsi Hua said:

"But those are just the qualities that we, your disciples, are unable to acquire."

ON OBSERVATION

Men's faults are characteristic. It is by observing a man's faults that one may come to know his virtues.

Observe a man's actions; scrutinize his motives; take note of the things that give him pleasure. How then can he hide from you what he really is?

Acquire new knowledge whilst thinking over the old, and you may become a teacher of others.

Study without thought is vain; thought (on Knowledge) without study is perilous.

Shall I tell you what true knowledge is? When you know, to know that you know, and when you do not know, to know that you do not know — that is true knowledge.

The scholar who is bent on studying the principles of virtue, yet is ashamed of bad clothes and coarse food, is not yet fit to receive instruction.

PROMINENCE

Instead of being concerned that you have no office, be concerned to think how you may fit yourself for office. Instead of being concerned that you are not known, seek to be worthy of being known.

SELF-CONTROL

When you see a good man, think of emulating him; when you see a bad man, examine your own heart.

Chi Wen Tzu used to reflect thrice before he acted. When told of this, the Master said: "Twice would do."

The Master said: "Alas! I have never seen a man who could see his own faults and arraign himself at the bar of his own conscience."

MEDITATION

Words of just admonition cannot fail to command a ready assent. But practical reformation is the thing that really matters. Words of kindly advice cannot fail to please the listener. But subsequent meditation on them is the thing that really matters.

I can make nothing of the man who is pleased with advice but will not meditate on it, who assents to admonition but does not reform.

LIFE AND DEATH

Chi Lu inquired concerning men's duty to spirits. The Master replied: "Before we are able to do our duty by the living, how can we do it by the spirits of the dead?" Chi Lu went on to inquire about death. The Master said: "Before we know what life is, how can we know what death is?"

RICH AND POOR

It is harder to be poor without murmuring than to be rich without arrogance.

VIRTUE FOR EFFECT

The men of olden time who studied virtue had only their own improvement in view; those who study it now have an eye to the applause of others.

ON TEACHING

Refusal to instruct one who is competent to learn entails the waste of a man. Instruction of one who is incompetent to learn entails waste of words. The wise man is he who wastes neither men nor words.

He who requires much from himself and little from others will be secure from hatred.

The real fault is to have faults and not try to amend them.

When a man is generally detested, or when he is generally beloved, closer examination is necessary.

Only two classes of men never change: The wisest of the wise and the dullest of the dull.

SHADOWS AND VIRTUES

Speaking to Tzu Lu, the Master said: "Have you ever heard of the six shadows which attend six great virtues?" "No," he replied. "Sit down then, and I will tell you. Love of goodness without the will to learn casts the shadow called foolishness. Love of knowledge without the will to learn casts the shadow called insensibility. Love of candor without the will to learn casts the shadow called rudeness. Love of daring without the will to learn casts the shadow called turbulence. Love of firmness without the will to learn casts the shadow called eccentricity."

Your goody-goody people are the thieves of virtue.

DOES GOD SPEAK

The Master said: "Would that I could do without speaking!" Tzu Kung said: "If our Master never spoke, how could we, his disciples, transmit his doctrines? "The Master replied: "Does God speak? The four seasons hold on their course, and all things continue to live and grow. Yet, tell me, does God speak?"

SERVANTS

Girls and servants are the most difficult people to handle. If you treat them familiarly, they become disrespectful; if you keep them at a distance, they resent it.

TRUE VALUES

When the solid outweighs the ornamental, we have boorishness; when the ornamental outweighs the solid, we have superficial smartness. Only from a proper blending of the two will the higher type of man emerge.

SAYINGS OF THE DISCIPLES

Tseng Tzu said: "Ability asking instruction of incompetence, abundance sitting at the feet of insufficiency, a man of every virtue who thought he had none, solid in character yet making himself a cipher, trespassed against but never retaliating, — such was the humble state of mind in which my late friend spent his life."

Tzu Hsia said: "The man who can appreciate moral worth and disengage his mind from sensual passion; who can put forth his utmost strength to serve his parents, and lay down his life to serve his prince; who speaks sincerely in his intercourse with friends — such a man, though the world may call him untaught, has in my opinion received the best and highest education."

Ssu-ma, lamenting, said: "All other men have brothers; I alone have none." Tzu Hsia said to him: "I have heard it said that life and death are divine dispensations, that wealth and rank depend on the will of God. The higher type of man is unfailingly attentive to his own conduct, and shows respect and true courtesy to others. Thus all within the world are his brethren. How then should he grieve at having no brothers?"

CONFUCIUS - THE DOCTRINE OF THE MEAN

ON TRUTH

Truth is the law of God. Acquired truth is the law of man. He who intuitively apprehends truth is one who, without effort, hits what is right, and without thinking understands what he wants to know; whose life is easily and naturally in harmony with the moral law. Such a one is what we call a saint or a man of divine nature. He who acquires truth is one who finds out what is good and holds fast to it.

In order to acquire truth, it is necessary to obtain a wide and extensive knowledge of what has been said and done in the world; critically to inquire into it; carefully to ponder over it; clearly to sift it; and earnestly to carry it out.

REALIZATION OF TRUTH

Truth means the realization of our being; and moral law means the law of our being. Truth is the beginning and end (the substance) of existence. Without truth there is no existence. It is for this reason that the moral man values truth.

Truth is not only the realization of our own being: it is that by which things outside of us have an existence. The realization of our being is moral sense. The realization of things outside of us is intellect. These, moral sense and intellect, are the powers and faculties of our being. They combine the inner and subjective and outer or objective use of the power of the mind. Therefore with truth everything done is right.

ABSOLUTE TRUTH

Thus absolute truth is indestructible. Being indestructible, it is eternal. Being eternal it is self-existent. Being self-existent, it is infinite. Being infinite it is vast and deep. Being vast and deep it is transcendental and intelligent.

It is because it is vast and deep that it contains all existence. It is because it is transcendental and intelligent that it embraces all existence. It is because it is infinite and eternal that it fills all existence.

In vastness and depth it is like the Earth. In transcendental intelligence it is like Heaven. Infinite and eternal, it is Infinitude itself.

Such being the nature of absolute truth, it manifests itself without being evident; it produces effects without action; it accomplishes its ends without being conscious.

TRUTH AND INTELLIGENCE

The intelligence which comes from the direct apprehension of truth is intuition. The apprehension of truth which comes from the exercise of intelligence is the result of education. Where there is truth, there is intelligence; where there is intelligence, there is truth.

TRUTH AND THE COSMIC LAWS

It is only he, in the world, who possesses absolute truth who can get to the bottom of the law of his being. He who is able to get to the bottom of the law of his being will be able to get to the bottom of the law of being of other men. He who is able to get to the bottom of the law of being of men will be able to get to the bottom of the laws of physical nature. He who is able to get to the bottom of the laws of physical nature will be able to influence the forces of creation of the Universe. He who can influence the forces of creation of the Universe is one with the Powers of the Universe.

TRUTH AND KNOWLEDGE

The next order of the process of man's mind is to attain to the apprehension of a particular branch of knowledge. In every particular branch of knowledge there is truth. Where there is truth, there is substance. Where there is substance, there is reality. Where there is reality, there is intelligence. Where there is intelligence, there is power. Where there is power there is influence. Where there is influence, there is creative power.

It is only he who possesses absolute truth in the world who can create.

TRUTH AND FOREKNOWLEDGE

It is an attribute of the possession of absolute truth to be able to foreknow. When a nation or family is about to flourish, there are sure to be lucky omens. When a nation or family is about to perish, there are sure to be signs and prodigies. These things manifest themselves in the instruments of divination and in the agitation of the human body. When happiness or calamity is about to come, it can be known beforehand. When it is good, it can be known beforehand. When it is evil, it can also be known beforehand.

Therefore he who possesses absolute truth is like a spiritual being.

MORAL LAW

I know now why there is no real moral life. The wise mistake moral law for something higher than what it really is; and the foolish do not know enough what moral law really is. I know now why the moral law is not understood. The noble natures want to live too high, high above their moral ordinary self; and ignoble natures do not live high enough, i.e., not up to their moral ordinary true self.

The life of the moral man is an exemplification of the universal moral order. The life of the vulgar person, on the other hand, is a contradiction of the universal moral order.

The moral law is a law from whose operation we cannot for one instant in our existence escape. A law from which we may escape is not the moral law. Wherefore it is that the moral man watches diligently over what his eyes cannot see and is in fear and awe of what his ears cannot hear. There is nothing more evident than that which cannot be seen by the eyes and nothing more palpable than that which cannot be perceived by the senses. Wherefore the moral man watches diligently over his secret thoughts.

Every system of moral laws must be based upon man's own consciousness. It must be verified by the common experience of men. Examined into by comparing it with the teachings of acknowledged great and wise men of the past, there must be no divergence. Applying it to the operations and processes of nature in the physical universe, there must be no contradiction. Confronted with the spiritual powers of the universe a man must be able to maintain it without any doubt. He must be prepared to wait a hundred generations after him for the coming of a man of perfect divine nature to confirm it without any misgiving.

FORCE OF CHARACTER

Force of character is a wonderful thing. Wherefore the man with the true force of moral character is one who is easy and accommodating and yet without weakness or indiscrimination. How unflinchingly firm he is in his strength! He is independent without any bias. When there is moral social order m the country, if he enters public life he does not change from what he was when in retirement. When there is no moral social order in the country he holds on his way without changing even unto death. How unflinchingly firm is he in his strengths

HOLDING TO THE MORAL LAW

There are men who seek for some abstruse meaning in religion and philosophy and live a life singular in order that they may leave a name to posterity. This is what I never would do. There are again good men who try to live in conformity with the moral law, but who, when they have gone halfway, throw it up. I never could give it up.

Lastly, there are truly more men who unconsciously live a life in entire harmony with the universal moral order and who live unknown to the world and unnoticed of men without any concern. It is only men of holy, divine natures who are capable of this.

UNDERSTANDING THE MORAL LAW

The moral law is to be found everywhere, and yet it is a secret. The simple intelligence of ordinary men and women of the people may understand something of the moral law; but in its utmost reaches there is something which even the holiest and wisest of men cannot understand.

The ignoble natures of ordinary men and women of the people may be able to carry out the moral law; but in its utmost reaches even the wisest and holiest of men cannot live up to it.

THE UNIVERSE AND THE MORAL MIND

Great as the Universe is, the man with the infinite moral nature in him is never satisfied.

For there is nothing so great but the mind of the moral man can conceive of something still greater which nothing in the world can hold. There is nothing so small but the mind of moral man can conceive of something still smaller which nothing in the universe can split. The Book of Songs says: "The hawk soars to the heavens above and fishes dive to the depths below." That is to say, there is no place in the highest heavens above nor in the deepest waters below where the moral law does not reign.

The moral law takes its rise in the relation between men and women; but in its utmost reaches it reigns supreme over heaven and earth.

PRACTICE OF THE MORAL LAW

The moral law is not something away from the actuality of human life. When men take up something away from the actuality of human life as the moral law, that is not the moral law. When a man carries out the principles of conscientiousness and reciprocity he is not far from the moral law. What you do not wish others should do unto you, do not do unto them.

FOUR POINTS OF THE MORAL LAW

There are four things in the moral life of a man not one of which I have been able to carry- out in my life. — To serve my father as I would expect my son to serve me: that I have not been able to do. To serve my sovereign as I would expect a minister under me to serve me: that I have not been able to do. To act toward my elder brother as I would expect my younger brother to act toward me: that I have not been able to do. To be the first to behave toward friends as I would expect them to behave toward me: that I have not been able to do.

IMPROVEMENT

In the discharge of the ordinary duties of life and in the exercise of care m ordinary conversation, whenever there is shortcoming, never fail to strive for improvement, and when there is much to be said, always say less than what is necessary; words having respect to actions and actions having respect to words. Is it not just this thorough genuineness and absence of pretense which characterizes the moral man?

SELF-CONTROL UNDER ALL CIRCUMSTANCES

The moral man conforms himself to his life circumstances; he does not desire anything outside of his position. Finding himself in a position of wealth and honor, he lives as becomes one living in a position of wealth and honor. Finding himself in a position of poverty and humble circumstances, he lives as becomes one living in a position of poverty and humble circumstances. Finding himself in uncivilized countries, he lives as becomes one living in uncivilized countries.

Finding himself in circumstances of danger and difficulty, he acts according to what is required of a man under such circumstances.

In one word, the moral man can find himself in no situation in life in which he is not master of himself.

In a high position he does not domineer over his subordinates. In a subordinate position he does not court the favors of his superiors. He puts in order his own personal conduct and seeks nothing from others; hence he has no complaint to make. He complains not against God nor rails against man.

Thus it is that the moral man lives out the even tenor of his life, calmly waiting for the appointment of God, whereas the vulgar person takes to dangerous courses, expecting the uncertain chances of luck.

SELF-ANALYSIS

In the practice of archery we have something resembling the principle in a man's moral life. When the archer misses the center of the target he turns round and seeks for the cause of his failure within himself.

BEGINNING AT THE BOTTOM

The moral life of man may be likened to traveling to a distant place: one must start from the nearest stage. It may also be likened to ascending a height: one must begin from the lowest step. The Book of Songs says:

"When wives and children and their sires are one,

'Tis like the harp and lute in unison.
When brothers live in concord and at peace
The strain of harmony shall never cease.
The lamp of happy union lights the home,
And bright days follow when the children come."

MORAL LAW AND NATURE

The moral laws form one system with the laws by which Heaven and Earth support and contain, overshadow and canopy all things. These moral laws form the same system with the laws by which the seasons succeed each other and the sun and moon appear with the alternations of day and night. It is this same system of laws by which all created things are produced and develop themselves each in its order and system without injuring one another; by which the operations of nature take their course without conflict and confusion, the lesser forces flowing everywhere like river currents, while the great forces of creation go silently and steadily on.

It is this — one system running through all — that makes the Universe so impressively great.

GIFTS OF THE MORALLY PERFECT

It is only the man with the most perfect divine moral nature who is able to combine in himself quickness of apprehension, intelligence, insight, and understanding: qualities necessary for the exercise of command; magnanimity, generosity, benignity, and gentleness: qualities necessary for the exercise of patience; originality, energy, strength of character, and determination: qualities necessary for the exercise of endurance; dignity, noble seriousness, order, and regularity: qualities necessary for the exercise of self-respect; grace, method, delicacy, and lucidity: qualities necessary for the exercise of critical judgment.

Thus all-embracing and vast is the nature of such a man. Profound it is and inexhaustible, like a living spring of water, ever running out with life and vitality. All-embracing and vast, it is like Heaven. Profound and inexhaustible, it is like the abyss.

As soon as such a man shall make his appearance in the world, all people shall reverence him. Whatever he says, all people will believe it. Whatever he does, all people will be pleased with it. Thus his name and fame will spread and fill all the civilized world, extending even to savage countries. Wherever ships and carriages reach; wherever the labor and enterprise of man penetrate; wherever the heavens overshadow and the earth sustains; wherever sun and moon shine; wherever frost and dew fall, all who have life and breath will honor him. Therefore we may say, "He is the equal of God."

When calamities or blessings are about to befall, the good or the evil will surely be foreknown to him. He, therefore, who is possessed of the completest sincerity, is like a spirit.

SPIRITUAL FORCES

The power of spiritual forces in the Universe — how active it is everywhere! Invisible to the eyes and impalpable to the senses, it is inherent in all things, and nothing can escape its operation.

It is a fact that there are these forces which make men in all countries fast and purify themselves, and with solemnity of dress institute services of sacrifice and religious worship. Like the rush of mighty waters, the presence of unseen Powers is felt, sometimes above us, sometimes around us.

The ordinance of God is what we call the law of our being. To fulfill the law of our being is what we call the moral law. The moral law when reduced to a system is what we call religion.

Confucius remarked: "There was the emperor Shun. He was perhaps what may be considered a truly great intellect. Shun had a natural curiosity of mind, and he loved to inquire into near facts [literally, "near words," meaning here ordinary topics of conversation in everyday life]. He looked upon evil merely as something negative; and he recognized only what was good as having a positive existence. Taking the two extremes of negative and positive, he applied the mean between the two extremes: in his judgment, employment, and dealings with people.

"This was characteristic of Shun's great intellect."

KNOWLEDGE OF MORALS

Some men are born with the knowledge of these moral qualities; some acquire it as the result of education; some acquire it as the result of hard experience. But when the knowledge is acquired, it comes to one and the same thing. Some exercise these moral qualities naturally and easily; some because they find it advantageous to do so; some with effort and difficulty. But when the achievement is made, it comes to one and the same thing.

When the passions, such as joy, anger, grief, and pleasure, have not awakened, that is our true self or moral being. When these passions awaken and each and ail attain due measure and degree, that is the moral order. Our true self or moral being is. the great reality [lit., "great root"] of existence, and moral order is the universal law in the world.

When true moral being and moral order are realized, the universe then becomes a cosmos and all things attain their full growth and development.

PERSONAL CONDUCT

By attending to the cleanliness and purity of his person and to the propriety and dignity of his dress, and in every word and act permitting nothing which is contrary to good taste and decency, that is how one puts in order his personal conduct.

THE FOOLISH

A man who is foolish, and yet is fond of using his own judgment; who is in humble circumstances, and yet is fond of assuming authority; who, while living in the present age, reverts to the ways of antiquity, such a man is one who will bring calamity upon himself.

LIFE OF THE MORAL MAN

The life of the moral man is plain and yet not unattractive; it is simple and yet full of grace; it is easy and yet methodical. He knows that accomplishment of great things consists in doing small things well. He knows that great effects are produced by small causes. He knows the evidence and reality of what cannot be perceived by the senses. Thus he is enabled to enter into the world of ideas and morals.

A man may be able to renounce the possession of kingdoms and empire, be able to spurn the honors and emoluments of office, be able to trample upon bare, naked weapons; with all that he shall not be able to find the central clue in his moral being.

Men all say, "We are wise"; but when driven forward and taken in a net, a trap, or a pitfall, there is not one who knows how to find a way of escape. Men all say, "We are wise"; but in finding the true central clue and balance in their moral being (i.e., their normal, ordinary, true self) and following the line of conduct which is in accordance with it, they are not able to keep it for a round month.

CONFUCIUS - THE GREAT LEARNING

The capacity for knowledge of the inferior man is small and easily filled up; the intelligence of the superior man is deep and not easily satisfied.

It matters not what you learn; but when you once learn a thing, you must never give it up until you have mastered it. It matters not what you inquire into; but when you inquire into a thing, you must never give it up until you have thoroughly understood it. It matters not what you try to think out; but when you once try to think out a thing, you must never give it up until you have got what you want. It matters not what you try to sift; but when you once try to sift out a thing, you must never give it up until you have sifted it out clearly and distinctly. It matters not what you try to carry out; but when you once try to carry out a thing, you must never give it up until you have done it thoroughly and well.

THE TRUE SCHOLAR

When the opportunity of gain is presented to him, he thinks on virtue. He is reverent in sacrifice; in mourning, absorbed in the sorrow he should feel. He who cherishes love of comfort is not fit to be a scholar.

The main object of study is to unfold the aim; with one who loves words, but does not improve, I can do nothing.

The scholar's burden is perfection; is it not heavy? It ends but with life; is it not enduring?

Learning is like raising a monument; if I stop with this basket of earth, it is my own fault. It is like throwing earth on the ground; one basket at a time, yet I advance.

The true scholar is not a mere utensil. Leaving Virtue without proper culture; failing thoroughly to discuss what is learned; being unable to move toward the righteousness of which knowledge is gained; and being unable to change what is not good, -these are the things that (in my scholars) give me anxiety.

If a man keeps cherishing his old knowledge, so as ever to acquire new, he may be a teacher of others. I marked Yen-Yuen's constant advance; I never saw him pause. Often the blade springs, but the plant does not go on to flower; often the plant flowers, but produces no fruit.

Having completed his studies, the scholar should devote himself to official functions. He should say: "I am not concerned that I have no place; I am concerned how I shall fit myself for one. I am not concerned at not being known; I seek to be worthy to be known."

MENCIUS. 371 B.C. - THE REAL MAN

A real man is one whose goodness is a part of himself. Of the qualities of the sage, none is greater than that of being a helper of men to right living. He is ashamed of a reputation beyond his desert. Having found the right way within himself, he rests in it, firm and serene, holding intimate converse with it, and reaching to its fountain-head. He obeys the right and waits for the appointed. His words are plain and simple, yet of widest bearing. His aim is self-culture, yet it gives peace to all men.

All things are already complete in us. There is no greater delight than to be conscious of right within us. If one strive to treat others as he would be treated by them, he shall not fail to come near the perfect life. Every duty is a charge, but the charge of oneself is the root of all others. The disease of men is to neglect their own fields and go to weeding those of others, to exact much from others and lay light burdens on themselves.

Over-readiness of speech comes of not having been reproved.

Even those who strive to be perfect stand in need of reproof.

A true scholar holds possession of himself, neither by riches nor poverty forced away from his virtue.

THE WARNING VOICE WITHIN

Let not a man do what his sense of right bids him not to do, nor desire what it forbids him to desire. This is sufficient. The skillful artist will not alter his measures for the sake of a stupid workman.

When right ways disappear, one's person must vanish with one's principles.

The honor which man confers is not true honor. Those to whom Chaou Mang gave rank, he can degrade again. He whose good name comes from what he is, needs no trappings.

The ancients cultivated the nobility of Heaven, leaving that of men to follow in its train. Serving Heaven consists in nourishing the real constitution of our being, anxious neither about death nor life.

THE DISCIPLINE OF HEAVEN

When Heaven is about to confer a great office on any man, it first disciplines his mind with suffering, and his bones and sinews with toil.

It exposes him to want and subjects him to extreme poverty.

It confounds his undertakings. By all these methods it stimulates his mind, hardens him, an supplies his incompetencies.

CONCERNING DESIRES

To nourish the heart there is nothing better than to make the desires few. Here is a man whose desires are few; in some things he may not be able to keep his heart, but they will be few. Here is a man whose desires are many; in some things he may be able to keep his heart, but they will be few.

THE CHILD-HEART

The great man is he who does not lose his child-heart. He does not think beforehand that his words shall be sincere, nor that his acts shall be resolute; he simply abides in the right.

The right path (Tao) is near, yet men seek it afar off.

The labor of duty is easy, yet men seek it in what is difficult.

The way is wide; it is not hard to know. Go home and seek it, and you shall not lack teachers.

EQUANIMITY

If one treat me unreasonably, I will say: "I must have been wanting in kindness or propriety. How else should this have happened?" Then I will mend my ways. If the other continue perverse, I must have self-respect enough to say, "I must have failed to do my best." If all is vain, I say, "Why vex myself about a wild beast?"

Thus the wise has lifelong vigilance, but not one morning's serious trouble.

THE END OF WISDOM IS TO SEEK THE LOST MIND

The virtues are not poured into us, they are natural: seek, and you will find them; neglect, and you will lose them. To every faculty and relation belongs its normal law; but without its fit culture it will decay. How lamentable to lose this mind and not know how to seek it!

Of all seeds their virtue is in their ripeness. Only he who has studied his mental constitution knows his nature; knowing his nature, he knows Heaven.

GREATNESS

They are great men who follow that part of them which is great. Let one stand in his nobler part, and the meaner will not be able to take it from him. This is simply what makes greatness. The superior man desires a wide sphere that he may give peace to multitudes; but what It's nature makes his own, cannot be greatened by the largeness of his sphere, nor lessened by its obscurity.

What is a good man? A man who commands our liking, is what is called a good man.

He whose goodness is part of himself, is what is called a real man.

He whose goodness has been filled up, is what is called a beautiful man.

He whose completed goodness is brightly displayed, is what is called a great man.

When this great man exercises a transforming influence, he is what is called a sage.

When the sage is beyond our knowledge, he is what is called a spirit-man.

Abstract good principles are not enough to give the kingdom peace; laws cannot execute themselves. If the good and wise be not trusted, the State will come to naught. The people are the most important element in a State; the ruler is the least. The empire is not given by one man to another. The choice of Heaven is shown in the conduct of men. It is an old rule that the oppressor may be put to death without warning. King Seuen asked about relatives of the ruler, when high ministers. Mencius replied that, if he had great faults and would not hear advice, they should dethrone him. The king changed countenance.

The disciple Kung-too said: "All are equally men, but some are great men, and some are little men; how is this?" Mencius replied: "Those who follow that part of themselves which is great are great men; those who follow that part which is little are little men."

Kung-too pursued: "All axe equally men, but some follow that part of themselves which is great, and some follow that part which is little; how is this?" Mencius answered: "The senses of hearing and seeing do not think, and are obscured by external things. When one thing comes into contact with another, as a matter of course it leads it away. To the mind belongs the office of thinking. By thinking, it gets the right view of things; by neglecting to think, it fails to do this.

"These, the senses and the mind, are what Heaven has given to us.

"Let a man first stand fast in the supremacy of the nobler part of his constitution, and the inferior part will not be able to take it from him. It is simply this which makes the great man."

THE WISE

The wise embrace all knowledge, but they are most earnest about what is of the greatest importance. The benevolent embrace all in their love, but what they consider of the greatest importance is to cultivate an earnest affection for the virtuous. Even the wisdom of Yaou and Shun did not extend to everything, but they attended earnestly to what was important.

Their benevolence did not show itself in acts of kindness to every man, but they earnestly cultivated an affection for the virtuous.

THE TRUE AND THE FALSE

I hate a semblance which is not the reality. I hate the darnel, lest it be confounded with the corn. I hate glib-tonguedness, lest it be confounded with righteousness. I hate sharpness of tongue, lest it be confounded with sincerity. I hate the music of Ch'ing, lest it be confounded with the true music. I hate the reddish blue, lest it be confounded with vermilion. I hate your good, careful men of the villages, lest they be confounded with the truly virtuous.

TRANSCENDENTALISM

Man does not live by experience alone, but by transcending experience, assured of what he does not see, and never has seen, as real; nor can he ever recognize the absolute worth and authority involved in the idea of duty but by a mental lift into a sphere above all the limits and contingencies of actual human conduct.

QUALITIES OF THE GREAT

To dwell in the wide house of the world; to stand in true attitude therein; to walk in the wide path of men; in success, to share one's principles with the people; m failure, to live them out alone; to be incorruptible by riches or honors, unchangeable by poverty, unmoved by perils or power, — these I call the qualities of a great man.

APPOINTMENTS OF THE GREAT

The exercise of love between father and son, the observance of righteousness between sovereign and minister, the rules of ceremony between guest and host, the display of knowledge m recognizing the talented, and the fulfilling the heavenly course by the sage, — these are the appointments of Heaven. But there is an adaptation of our nature for them. The superior man does not say in reference to them, "It is the appointment of Heaven."

For the mouth to desire sweet tastes, the eye to desire beautiful colors, the ear to desire pleasant sounds, the nose to desire fragrant odors, and the four limbs to desire rest and ease, — these things are natural. But there is an appointment of Heaven in connection with them, and the superior man does not say of his pursuit of them, "It is my nature."

In the empire there are three things universally acknowledged to be honorable. Nobility is one of them, age is one of them, virtue is one of them.

In courts nobility holds first place, in villages age, and for usefulness to one's generation, and controlling the people, neither is equal to virtue.

When one subdues men by force, they do not submit to him in heart but because not strong enough to resist. When one subdues men by virtue, they are pleased to the heart's core and sincerely submit.

RESPONSIBILITIES OF THE GOVERNMENT

When men die of famine, you say it is the season that is to blame. What does this differ from saying, when you have caused a man's death. "It was not I, but the weapon"?

"When a public officer is neglectful, what would you do with him?"

"Cast him off," replies the king.

"When in the whole kingdom there is no good government, what then?"

King Seuen looked to the right and left, and spoke of other matters.

When the old and weak are found lying in ditches, and your granaries are full, and none of your prefects has told you of these things, do not blame the people that they seize their opportunity to repay such treatment!

If you know a tax to be unjust, end it at once!

Man has ten thousand plans for himself; God but one for him. Man cries, "Now, now!" God says, "Not yet, not yet."

A good man protects three villages.

Let your ideas be round and your conduct square.

Right heart need not fear evil seeming.

God drives no man to despair.

One day of wedded life deserves a hundred days of kindness.

Misfortunes issue where diseases enter, — at the mouth.

What is whispered in the ear is heard miles away.

The gods cannot help one who loses opportunities.

Dig your well before you are thirsty.

Swim with one foot on the ground.

Forbearance is the jewel of home.

A great man never loses the simplicity of a child.

Prefer right to kindred (in patronage).

He who soars not, suffers not by a fall.

If you receive an ox, give back a horse.

Act with kindness, but do not exact gratitude.

Give by day, and your reward shall spring by night.

By virtue alone in itself, one never reaches rule over men's hearts.

He must make his virtue sustain others.

Good-will subdues its opposite, as water fire.

Friendship with a man is friendship with his virtue.

A people's limits do not consist in dikes and borders. The security of a State is not in the strength of mountains and streams. No advantages compare with the accord of men.

They who expect to live without enemies, yet have no kindness for others, are like one who should try to hold a heated body without dipping it in water.

Men expect by their own darkness to enlighten others. The artisan may give a man compass and square, but he cannot make him skillful in the use of them.

What misery they shall suffer who talk of the evil in others. A man must first despise himself, then others will despise him. A family must first overthrow itself, then others will overthrow it. A State must first smite itself, then others will smite it.

Incessant falls teach men to reform, and distresses rouse their strength.

Life springs from calamity, and death from ease. Men of special virtue and wisdom are wont to owe these powers to the trials they have endured.

If you have not passed the bitterness of starvation, you know not the blessings of abundance; if not through the parting of death, you know not the joy of unbroken union; if not through calamity, the pleasure of security; if not through storms, the luxury of calm.

The white clouds pass; the blue heaven abides. Noble natures are calm and content. The song of a dying bird is plaintive; the words of a dying man are just.

How can man reward the care of Heaven?

Mock not, O young man, at gray hairs! How long can the opening flower keep its bloom?

The wise place virtue in thought.

A good word has heat enough for three winters; a hard one wounds like six months of cold. To yield to Heaven is to save one's self.

If there is too much rice in the kitchen, there are starving people on the road. To help another helps yourself. Drink less and learn more. The spirits know your secret sins.

Kwan said: "Now the whole kingdom is drowning; how is it that you do not save it?" Mencius replied: "A drowning kingdom must be rescued by right principles, not like a drowning person, by the hand."

Have you watched the growing grain after the season of drought, how, when the rain falls, it stands up refreshed? Who can keep it back? These shepherds of men all love to destroy men. Were there but one who did not, the people would hasten to obey him as rushing waters that cannot be stayed.

"Venerable man," said the king, "since you have come here a distance of a thousand Ii, you have doubtless something to say for the profit of my kingdom." Mencius replied: "O King, why talk of profit? I have humanity and justice for my teaching, nothing more. If these be put last, and profit first, your officers will not be content till they have stripped you of all."

The wise questions himself, the fool others.

When the prince goes to school, he is like other boys.

The highest official is subject to the law.

Whoso is too subservient to masters will reap shame.

A good subject cannot serve two masters; lay not two saddles on one horse.

A minister who fears death will not be faithful.

Judge not by appearance; the sea cannot be scooped up in a tumbler.

Think reasonably, be strong for virtue, lean on humanity, and in all things be content.

LAO TZU. 604 B.C. - FROM THE TAO-TEH KING

The grandest forms of active force
From Tao come, their only source.
Who can of Tao the nature tell?
Our sight it flies, our touch as well.

The Tao that can be trodden is not the enduring and unchanging Tao.

He who knows the Tao does not care to speak about it; he who is ever ready to speak about it does not know it.

Those who know the Tao are not extensively learned; the extensively learned do not know it.

The relation of Tao to all the world is like that of the great rivers and seas to the streams from the valleys.

The Tao which can be expressed in words is not the eternal Tao; the name which can be uttered is not its eternal name. Without a name, it is the beginning of Heaven and Earth; with a name, it is the Mother of all things.

Only one who is eternally free from earthly passions can apprehend its spiritual essence; he who is ever clogged by passions can see no more than its outer form.

THE SPIRITUAL AND MATERIAL

These two things, the spiritual and the material, though we call them by different names, in their origin are one and the same. This sameness is a mystery, — the mystery of mysteries. It is the gate of all spirituality.

Tao eludes the sense of sight and is therefore called colorless.

It eludes the sense of hearing and is therefore called soundless.

It eludes the sense of touch and is therefore called incorporeal.

These three qualities cannot be apprehended, and hence they may be blended into unity.

THE FORM OF TAO

Its upper part is not bright, and its lower part is not obscure.

Ceaseless in action, it cannot be named, but returns again to nothingness.

We may call it the form of the formless, the image of the imageless, the fleeting and the indeterminable.

Would you go before it, you cannot see its face; would you go behind it, you cannot see its back.

THE FORCE OF TAO

The mightiest manifestations of active force flow solely from Tao.

Tao in itself is vague, impalpable, — how impalpable, how vague! Yet within it there is Substance.

How profound, how obscure! Yet within it there is a vital Principle. This Principle is the Quintessence of Reality, and out of it comes Truth,

From of old until now, its name has never passed away. It watches over the beginning of all things.

How do I know this about the beginning of things? Through Tao.

THE INFINITE

There is something, chaotic yet complete, which existed before Heaven and Earth. Oh, how still it is and formless, standing alone without changing, reaching everywhere without suffering harm!

It must be regarded as the Mother of the Universe. Its name I know not.

To designate it I call it Tao. Endeavoring to describe it, I call it great.

THE GREATNESS OF TAO

Therefore Tao is great; Heaven is great; the Earth is great; and the Sovereign also is great.

In the Universe there are four powers, of which the Sovereign is one.

Man takes his law from the Earth; the Earth takes its law from Heaven; Heaven takes its law from Tao; but the law of Tao is its own spontaneity.

THE UNCHANGING TAO

Tao in its unchanging aspect has no name. Small though it be in its primordial simplicity, mankind dare not claim its service. Could princes and kings hold and keep it, all creation would spontaneously pay homage. Heaven and Earth would unite in sending down sweet dew, and the people would be righteous unbidden and of their own accord.

All-pervading is the Great Tao. It can be at once on the right hand and on the left. All things depend on it for life, and it rejects them not.

Its task accomplished, it takes no credit. It loves and nourishes all things, but does not act as master. It is ever free from desire. We may call it small. All things return to it, yet it does not act as master.

We may call it great.

The whole world will flock to him who holds the mighty form of Tao. They will come and receive no hurt, but find rest, peace, and tranquillity.

Tao is a great square with no angles, a great vessel which takes long to complete, a great sound which cannot be heard, a great image with no form.

HIGHEST AND LOWEST

The highest goodness is like water, for water is excellent in benefiting all things, and it does not strive. It occupies the lowest place, which men abhor. And therefore it is near akin to Tao.

NATURAL LAW AND TAO

All things alike do their work, and then we see them subside. When they have reached their bloom, each returns to its origin. Returning to their origin means rest or fulfillment of destiny. This reversion is an eternal law. To know that law is to be enlightened. Not to know it, is misery and calamity. He who knows the eternal law is liberal-minded. Being liberal-minded, he is just. Being just, he is kingly. Being kingly, he is akin to Heaven. Being akin to Heaven, he possesses Tao. Possessed of Tao, he endures forever. Though his body perish, yet he suffers no harm.

THE FIRST CAUSE

The world has a first cause, which may be regarded as the Mother of the World. When one has the Mother, one can know the Child. He who knows the Child and still keeps the Mother, though his body perish, shall run no risk of harm.

THE WAY OF HEAVEN

It is the way of Heaven not to strive, and yet it knows how to overcome; not to speak, and yet it knows how to obtain a response; it calls not, and things come of themselves; it is slow to move, but excellent in its designs.

It is the way of Heaven to take from those who have too much and give to those who have too little. But the way of man is not so. He takes away from those who have too little, to add to his own superabundance.

What man is there who can take of his own superabundance and give it to mankind? Only he who possesses Tao.

ON SELF-ASSERTION

He who is self-approving does not shine. He who boasts has no merit. He who exalts himself does not rise high. Judged according to Tao, he is like remnants of food or a tumor on the body, — an object of universal disgust. Therefore one who has Tao will not consort with such.

ON PERFECT VIRTUE

Perfect Virtue acquires nothing, therefore it obtains everything. Perfect Virtue does nothing, yet there is nothing which it does not effect.

Perfect Charity operates without the need of anything to evoke it.

Perfect Duty to one's neighbor operates, but always needs to be evoked.

Perfect Ceremony operates and calls for no outward response, nevertheless it induces respect.

Knowledge is but a showy ornament of Tao, while ofttimes the beginning of imbecility.

THE SUPERIOR SCHOLAR

When the superior scholar hears of Tao, he diligently practices it. When the average scholar hears of Tao, he sometimes retains it, sometimes loses it. When the inferior scholar hears of Tao, he loudly laughs at it. Were it not thus ridiculed, it would not be worthy of the name of Tao.

DISPLAY

The wearing of gay, embroidered robes, thc carrying of sharp swords, fastidiousness in food and drink, superabundance of property and wealth,'—this I call flaunting robbery; most assuredly it is not Tao.

BEGIN HARMONY WITH YOUR AGE

Temper your sharpness, disentangle your ideas, moderate your brilliance, live in harmony with your age. This is being in conformity with the principle of Tao. Such a man is impervious alike to favor and disgrace, to benefits and injuries, to honor and contempt. And therefore he is esteemed above all mankind.

MODERATION IN GOVERNMENT

In governing men and serving Heaven there is nothing like moderation. For only by moderation can there be an early return to man's normal state. This early return is the same as a great storage of Virtue. With a great storage of Virtue there is naught that may not be achieved. If there is naught which may not be achieved, then no one will know to what extent this power reaches. And if no one knows to what extent a man's power reaches, that man is fit to be the ruler of a State. Having the secret of rule, his rule shall endure. Setting the taproot deep and making the spreading roots firm, this is the way to insure long life to the tree.

ANCIENT PHILOSOPHERS

The skillful philosophers of the olden time were subtle, spiritual, profound, and penetrating. They were so deep as to be incomprehensible. Because they are hard to comprehend, I will endeavor to describe them.

Shrinking were they, like one fording a stream in winter. Cautions were they, like one who fears an attack from any quarter. Circumspect were they, like a stranger guest; self-effacing, like ice about to melt; simple, like unpolished wood; vacant, like a valley; opaque, like muddy water.

ON THE NATURE OF THINGS

Among mankind the recognition of beauty as such implies the idea of ugliness, and the recognition of good implies the idea of evil.

There is the same mutual relation between existence and non-existence in the matter of creation; between difficulty and ease in the matter of accomplishing; between long and short in the matter of form; between high and low in the matter of elevation; between treble and bass in the matter of musical pitch; between fore and after in the matter of priority.

Nature is not benevolent; with ruthless indifference she makes all things serve their purposes, like the straw dogs we use at sacrifices. The sage is not benevolent; he utilizes the people with the like inexorability.

Heaven and Earth are long-lasting. The reason why Heaven and Earth can last long is that they live not for themselves, and thus they are able to endure.

Thirty spokes unite in one nave; the utility of the cart depends on the hollow center in which the axle turns. Clay is molded into a vessel; the utility of the vessel depends on its hollow interior. Doors and windows are cut out in order to make a house; the utility of the house depends on the empty spaces.

Thus, while the existence of things may be good, it is the non-existent in them which makes them serviceable.

Cast off your holiness, rid yourself of sagacity, and the people will benefit a hundredfold. Discard benevolence and abolish righteousness, and people will return to filial piety and paternal love. Renounce your scheming, and abandon gain, and thieves and robbers will disappear.

These three precepts mean that outward show is insufficient, and therefore they bid us be true to our proper nature, to show simplicity, to embrace plain dealing, to reduce selfishness to moderate desire.

He who knows others is clever, but he who knows himself is enlightened.

He who overcomes others is strong, but he who overcomes himself is mightier still.

He is rich who knows when he has enough.

He who acts with energy has strength of purpose.

He who moves not from his proper place is long-lasting.

He who dies, but perishes not, enjoys true longevity.

If you would contract, you must first expand. '
If you would weaken, you must first strengthen.
If you would overthrow, you must first raise up.
If you would take, you must first give.
This is called the dawn of intelligence.

He who is most perfect, seems to be lacking; yet his resources are never outworn.

He who is most full seems vacant; yet his uses are inexhaustible.

Extreme straightness is as bad as crookedness. Extreme cleverness is as bad as folly. Extreme fluency is as bad as stammering.

Those who know do not speak; those who speak do not know.

He who acts, destroys; he who grasps, loses. Therefore the Sage does not act, and so does not destroy; he does not grasp, and so he does not lose.

The Sage does not care to hoard. The more he uses for the benefit of others, the more he possesses himself. The more he gives to his fellow-men, the more he has of his own.

LAO TZU - WU-WEI

Do nothing by self-will, but rather conform to the Infinite Will, and everything will be done for you.

Who is there that can make muddy water clear? But if allowed to remain still, it will become clear of itself. Who is there that can secure a state of absolute repose? But let time go on, and the state of repose will gradually arise.

Tao is eternally inactive, and yet it leaves nothing undone. If the princes and kings could but hold fast to this principle, all things would work out their own reformation. If, having reformed, they still desire to act, I would have them restrained by the simplicity of the Nameless Tao.

The simplicity of the Nameless Tao brings about an absence of desire. The absence of desire gives tranquillity. And thus the empire will rectify itself.

The softest things in the world override the hardest. That which has no substance enters where there is no crevice. Hence I know the advantage of inaction.

Without going out of doors, one may know the whole world; without looking out of the window, one may see the Way of Heaven. The further one travels, the less one may know. Thus it is that without moving you shall know, without looking you shall see, without doing you shall achieve.

The pursuit of book learning brings about daily increase. The practice of Tao brings about daily loss. Repeat this loss again and again, and you arrive at inaction. Practice inaction, and there is nothing which cannot be done.

Desire not to desire, and you will not value things difficult to obtain. Learn not to learn, and you will revert to a condition which mankind in general has lost.

Leave all things to take their natural course, and do not interfere.

ON SELF-DISPLAY

All things in nature work silently. They come into being and possess nothing. They fulfill their functions and make no claim.

When merit has been achieved, do not take it to yourself; for if you do not take it to yourself, it shall never be taken from you.

Keep behind, and you shall be put in front; keep out, and you shall be kept in.

Goodness strives not, and therefore it is not rebuked.

He that humbles himself shall be preserved entire. He that bends shall be made straight.

He that is empty shall be filled. He that is worn out shall be renewed. He who has little shall succeed. He who has much shall go astray.

He who, conscious of being strong, is content to be weak, — he shall be the paragon of mankind.

Being the paragon of mankind, Virtue will never desert him. He returns to the state of a little child.

He who, conscious of his own light, is content to be obscure, — he shall be the whole world's model; his Virtue will never fail. He reverts to the Absolute.

He who is great, must make humility his base. He who is high, must make lowliness his foundation. Thus princes and kings in speaking of themselves use the terms "lonely," "friendless," "of small account." Is not this making humility their base?

Thus it is said that "Some things are increased by being diminished, others are diminished by being increased." What others have taught, I also teach; verily, I will make it the root of my teaching.

Therefore the Sage, wishing to be above the people, must by his words put himself below them; wishing to be before the people, he must put himself behind them. In this way, though he has his place above them, people do not feel his weight; though he has his place before them, they do not feel it an injury. Therefore all mankind delight to exalt him, and weary of him not.

I have three precious things which I hold fast and prize. The first is gentleness; the second is frugality; the third is humility, which keeps me from putting myself before others. Be gentle, and you can be bold; be frugal, and you can be liberal; avoid putting yourself before others, and you can become a leader among men.

Gentleness brings victory to him who attacks, and safety to him who defends. Those whom Heaven would save, it fences round with gentleness.

The best soldiers are not warlike; the best fighters do not lose their temper. The greatest conquerors are those who overcome their enemies without strife. The greatest directors of men are those who yield place to others. This is called the Virtue of not striving, the capacity for directing mankind; this is being the compeer of Heaven. It was the highest goal of the ancients.

ON RULING THE PEOPLE

Not exalting worth keeps the people from rivalry. Not prizing what is hard to procure keeps the people from theft. Not to show them what they may covet is the way to keep their minds from disorder.

He who respects the State as his own person is fit to govern it. He who loves the State as his own body is fit to be intrusted with it.

In the highest antiquity, the people did not know that they had rulers. In the next age, they loved and praised them. In the next, they feared them. In the next, they despised them.

As restrictions and prohibitions are multiplied in the empire, the people grow poorer and poorer. When the people are subjected to overmuch government, the land is thrown into confusion. When the people are skilled in many cunning arts, strange are the objects of luxury that appear.

The greater the number of laws and enactments, the more thieves and robbers there will be. Therefore the Sage says: "So long as I do nothing, the people will work out their own reformation. So long as I love calm, the people will right themselves. If only I keep from meddling, the people will grow rich. If only 1 am free from desire, the people will come naturally back to desire."

Do not confine the people within too narrow bounds; do not make their lives too weary. For if you do not weary them of life, they will not then grow weary of you.

Were I ruler of a little State with a small population, with only ten or a hundred men available as soldiers, I would not use them. I would have the people look on death as a grievous thing, and they should not travel to distant countries. Though they might possess boats and carriages, they should have no occasion to ride in them. Though they might own weapons and armor, they should have no need to use them. I would make people return to the use of knotted cords. They should find their plain food sweet, their rough garments fine. They should be content with their simple homes, and happy in their simple ways. If a neighboring State was within sight of mine — nay, if we were close enough to hear the crowing of each other's cocks and the barking of each other's dogs — the two peoples should grow old and die without there ever having been any mutual intercourse.

LAO TZU - PRECEPTS AND SAYINGS

By many words wit is exhausted; it is better to preserve a mean.

He who grasps more than he can hold, would be better without any.

If a house is crammed with treasures of gold and jade, it will be impossible to guard them all.

The excellence of a dwelling is in its site; the excellence of a mind in its profundity; the excellence of giving is charitableness; the excellence of speech is truthfulness; the excellence of government is order; the excellence of action is ability; the excellence of movement is timeliness.

He who prides himself upon wealth and honor hastens his own downfall.

He who strikes with a sharp point will not himself be safe for long.

He who embraces unity of soul by subordinating animal instincts to reason will be able to escape" dissolution. He who strives his utmost after tenderness can become even as a little child.

If a man is clear-headed and intelligent, can he be without knowledge?

The Sage attends to the inner and not to the outer; he puts away the objective and holds to the subjective.

Between yes and yea, how small the difference!

Between good and evil, how great the difference!

What the world reverences may not be treated with respect.

He who has no faith in others shall find no faith in them.

To see oneself is to be clear of sight. Mighty is he who conquers himself.

He who raises himself on tiptoe cannot stand firm; he who stretches his legs wide apart cannot walk.

Racing and hunting excite man's heart to madness.

The struggle for rare possessions drives a man to actions injurious to himself.

The heavy is the foundation of the light; repose is the ruler of unrest.

The wise prince in his daily course never departs from gravity and repose. Though he possess a gorgeous palace, he will dwell therein with calm indifference. How should the lord of a million chariots conduct himself in the empire? Levity loses men's hearts; unrest loses the throne.

The skillful traveler leaves no tracks; the skillful speaker makes no blunders; the skillful reckoner uses no tallies. He who knows how to shut, uses no bolts; yet you cannot open. He who knows how to bind, uses no cords; yet you cannot undo.

Among men, reject none; among things, reject nothing. This is called comprehensive intelligence.

The good man is the bad man's teacher; the bad man is the material upon which the good man works. If the one does not value his teacher, if the other does not love his material, then despite their sagacity they must go far astray. This is a mystery of great import.

The course of things is such that what was in front is now behind; what was hot is now cold; what was strong is now weak; what was complete is now in ruin. Therefore the Sage avoids excess, extravagance, and grandeur.

Which is nearer to you, fame or life? Which is more to you, life or wealth? Which is the greater malady, gain or loss?

Excessive ambitions necessarily entail great sacrifices. Much hoarding must be followed by heavy loss. He who knows when he has enough will not be put to shame. Such a man can look forward to long life.

There is no sin greater than ambition; no calamity greater than discontent; no vice more sickening than covetousness. He who is content, always has enough.

Do not wish to be rare like jade, nor common like stone.

The Sage has no hard and fast ideas, but he shares the ideas of the people and makes them his own. Living in the world, he is apprehensive lest his heart be sullied by contact with the world. The people all fix their eyes and ears upon him. The Sage looks upon all as his children.

I have heard that he who possesses the secret of life, when traveling abroad, will not flee from rhinoceros or tiger; when entering a hostile camp, he will not equip himself with sword or buckler. The rhinoceros finds in him no place to insert his horn; the tiger has nowhere to fasten its claw; the soldier has nowhere to thrust his blade. And why? Because he has no spot where death can enter.

To see small beginnings is clearness of sight. To rest in weakness is strength.

He who knows how to plant, shall not have his plant uprooted; he who knows how to hold a thing, shall not have it taken away. Sons and grandsons shall worship at his shrine, which shall endure for generations.

Knowledge in harmony is called constant. Constant knowledge is called wisdom. Increase of life is called felicity. The mind directing the body is called strength.

Be square without being angular. Be honest without being mean. Be upright without being punctilious. Be brilliant without being showy.

Good words shall gain you honor in the marketplace, but good deeds shall gain you friends among men.

To the good I would be good; to the not-good I would also be good in order to make them good.

With the faithful I would keep faith; with the unfaithful I would also keep-.faith, in order that they may become faithful.

Even if a man is bad, how can it be right to cast him off?

Requite injury with kindness.

The difficult things of this world must once have been easy; the great things of this world must once have been small. Set about difficult things while they are still easy; do great things while they are still small.

The Sage never affects to do anything great, and therefore he is able to achieve his great results.

He who always thinks things easy, is sure to find them difficult. Therefore the Sage ever anticipates difficulties, and thus it is he never encounters them.

While times are quiet, it is easy to take action; ere coming troubles have cast their shadows, it is easy to lay plans.

That which is brittle is easily broken; that which is minute is easily dissipated. Take precautions before the evil appears; regulate things before disorder has begun.

The tree which needs two arms to span its girth sprang from the tiniest shoot. Yon tower, nine stories high, rose from a little mound of

earth. A journey of a thousand miles began with a single step.

The Sage knows what is in him, but makes no display; he respects himself, but seeks not honor for himself.

To know, but to be as though not knowing, is the height of wisdom. Not to know and yet to affect knowledge, is a vice. If we regard this vice as such, we shall escape it.

The Sage has not this vice. It is because he regards it as a vice that he escapes it.

Use the light that is in you to revert to your natural clearness of sight. Then the loss of the body is unattended with calamity. This is called doubly enduring.

In the management of affairs, people constantly break down just when they are nearing a successful issue. If they took as much care at the end as at the beginning, they would not fail in their enterprises.

He who lightly promises, is sure to keep but little faith.

He whose boldness leads him to venture, will be slain; he who is brave enough not to venture, will live. Of these two, one has the benefit, the other has the hurt. But who is it that knows the real cause of Heaven's hatred? This is why the Sage hesitates and finds it difficult to act.

The violent and stiff-necked die not by a natural death.

True words are not fine; fine words are not true.

CHUANG TZU. 400 B. C - . RIGHT AND WRONG

Those who would have right without its correlative, wrong, or good government without its correlative, misrule, — they do not apprehend the great principles of the universe nor the conditions to which all creation is subject. One might as well talk of the existence of heaven without that of earth, or of the negative principle without the positive, which is clearly absurd.

THE TRUE STANDARD

If you adopt, as absolute, a standard of evenness which is so only relatively, your results will not be absolutely even. If you adopt, as absolute, a criterion of right which is so only relatively, your results will not be absolutely right. Those who trust to their senses become slaves to objective existences. Those alone who are guided by their intuitions find the true standard. So far are the senses less reliable than the intuitions. Yet fools trust to their senses to know what is good for mankind, with alas! but external results.

ON CONSCIOUSNESS

A drunken man who falls out of a cart, though he may suffer, does not die. His bones are the same as other people's, but he meets his accident in a different way. His spirit is in a condition of security. He is not conscious of riding in the cart; neither is he conscious of falling out of it. Ideas of life, death, fear, etc., cannot penetrate his breast; and so he does not fear from contact with objective existences.

And if such security is to be got from wine, how much more is it to be got from God? It is in God that the Sage seeks his refuge, and so he is free from harm.

KNOWLEDGE AND ATTAINMENT

He who knows what God is, and who knows what man is, has attained. Knowing what God is, he knows that he himself proceeded therefrom. Knowing what man is, he rests in the knowledge of the known, waiting for the knowledge of the unknown. Working out one's allotted span, and not perishing in mid-career, — this is the fullness of knowledge.

Herein, however, there is a flaw. Knowledge is dependent upon fulfillment, and as this fulfillment is uncertain, how can it be known that my divine is not really human, my human really divine?

We must have pure men, and then only can we have pure knowledge.

THE NATURAL ORDER

A man must go wheresoever his parents bid him. Nature is no other than a man's parents. If she bid me die quickly, and I demur, then I am an unfilial son. She can do me no wrong. Tao gives me this form, this toil in manhood, this repose in old age, this rest in death. And surely, that which is such a kind arbiter of my life is the best arbiter of my death.

How do I know that love of life is not a delusion after all? How do I know but that he who dreads to die is as a child who has lost its way and cannot find its home?

THE SOUL

But whether or not we ascertain what are the functions of this soul, it matters but little to the soul itself. For, coming into existence with this mortal coil of mine, with the exhaustion of this mortal coil its mandate will also be exhausted. To be harassed by the wear and tear of life, and to pass rapidly through it without possibility of arresting one's course, — is this not pitiful indeed? To labor without ceasing, and then, without living to enjoy the fruit, worn out, to depart suddenly, one knows not whither, — is not that a just cause for grief?

OBJECTIVE AND SUBJECTIVE

What advantage is there in what men call not dying? The body decomposes and the mind goes with it. This is our real cause for sorrow. Can the world be so dull as not to see this? Or is it I alone who am dull, and others not so?... There is nothing which is not objective; there is nothing which is not subjective. But it is impossible to start from the objective. Only from subjective knowledge is it possible to proceed to objective knowledge. Hence it has been said: "The objective emanates from the subjective; the subjective is consequent upon the objective. This is the Alternation Theory." Nevertheless, when one is born, the other dies. When one is possible, the other is impossible. When one is affirmative, the other is negative. Which being the case, the true Sage rejects all distinctions of this and that. He takes his refuge in God, and places himself in subjective relation with all things.

ON LIFE AND DEATH

Life follows upon death. Death is the beginning of life. Who knows when the end is reached? The life of man results from convergence of the vital fluid. Its convergence is life; its dispersion, death. If, then, life and death are but consecutive states, what need have I to complain?

Therefore all things are One. What we love is animation. What we hate is corruption. But corruption in its turn becomes animation, and animation once more becomes corruption.

Predestination involves a real existence. Chance implies an absolute absence of any principle. To have a name and the embodiment thereof, — this is to have a material existence. To have no name and no embodiment, — of this one can speak and think; but the more one speaks, the farther off one gets.

The unborn creature cannot be kept from life. The dead cannot be tracked. From birth to death is but a span; yet the secret cannot be known. Chance and predestination are but a priori solutions.

INFINITE

When I seek for a beginning, I find only time infinite. When I look forward to an end, I see only time infinite. Infinity of time past and* to come implies no beginning and is in accordance with the laws of material existences. Predestination and Chance give us a beginning, but one which is compatible only with the existence of matter.

A man's knowledge is limited; but it is upon what he does not know that he depends to extend his knowledge to the apprehension of God.

The ultimate end is God. He is manifested in the laws of nature. He is the hidden spring. At the beginning he was. This, however, is inexplicable. It is unknowable. But from the unknowable we reach the known.

A vulgar proverb says that he who has heard but part of the truth thinks no one equal to himself. And such a one am I.

"When formerly I heard people detracting from the learning of Confucius or underrating the heroism of Poh I, I did not believe. But now that I have looked upon your inexhaustibility — alas for me! had I not reached your abode, I should have been forever a laughingstock to those of comprehensive enlightenment!"

To which the Spirit of the Ocean replied: "You cannot speak of ocean to a well-frog, the creature of a narrower sphere. You cannot speak of ice to a summer insect, a creature of a season. You cannot speak of Tao to a pedagogue; his scope is too restricted. But now that you have emerged from your narrow sphere and have seen the great ocean, you know your own insignificance, and I can speak to you of great principles."

FINALITY

Dimensions are limitless; time is endless. Conditions are not invariable; terms are not final. Thus the wise man looks into space, and does not regard the small as too little, nor the great as too much; for he knows that there is no limit to dimension. He looks back into the past, and does not grieve over what is far off, nor rejoice over what is near; for he knows that time is without end. He investigates fullness and decay, and does not rejoice if he succeeds, nor lament if he fails; for he knows that conditions are not invariable. He who clearly apprehends the scheme of existence does not rejoice over life, nor repine at death; for he knows that terms are not final.

NATURAL INSTINCTS

The people have certain natural instincts: to weave and clothe themselves, to till and feed themselves. These are common to all humanity, and all are agreed thereon. Such instincts are called "Heaven-sent."

And so in the days when natural instincts prevailed, men moved quietly and gazed steadily. At that time, there were no roads over mountains, nor boats, nor bridges over water. AH things were produced, each for its own proper sphere. Birds and beasts multiplied; trees and shrubs grew up.

The former might be led by the hand; you could climb up and peep in the raven's nest. For then man dwelt with birds and beasts, and all creation was one.

There were no distinctions of good and bad men. Being all equally without knowledge, their virtue could not go astray.

Being all equally without evil desires, they were in a state of natural integrity, the perfection of human existence.

But when Sages appeared, tripping up people over charity and fettering them with duty to their neighbor, doubt found its way into the world.

And then, with their gushing over music and fussing over ceremony, the empire became divided against itself.

When Chuang Tzu was about to die, his disciples expressed a wish to give him a splendid funeral. But Chuang Tzu said: "With heaven and earth for my coffin and shell; with the sun, moon, and stars as my burial regalia; and with all creation to escort me to the grave, — are not my funeral paraphernalia ready to hand?"

"We fear," argued the disciples, "lest the carrion kite should eat the body of our master;" to which Chuang Tzu replied: "Above ground I shall be food for kites; below I shall be food for mole-crickets and ants. Why rob one to feed the other?"

A man who knows that he is a fool is not a great fool.

A dog is not considered a good dog because he is a good barker. A man is not considered a good man because he is a good talker.

Get rid of small wisdom, and great wisdom will shine upon you.

Put away goodness, and you will be naturally good. A child does not learn to speak because taught by professors of the art, but because it lives among people who can themselves speak.

The best language is that which is not spoken, the best form of action is that which is without deeds.

Spread out your knowledge, and it will be found to be shallow.

The perfect man ignores self; the divine man ignores action; the true Sage ignores reputation.

SEVERANCE

The perfect man is a spiritual being. Were the ocean itself scorched up, he would not feel hot. Were the Milky Way frozen hard, he would not feel cold. Were the mountains to be riven with thunder, and the great deep to be thrown up by storm, he would not tremble.

Birth is not a beginning; death is. not an end.

Let knowledge stop at the unknowable. That is perfection.

YANG CHU. 300 B.C. - FAME AND VANITY

Yang Chu, when traveling in Lu, put up at Meng Sun Yang's.

Meng asked him: "A man can never be more than a man; why do people still trouble themselves about fame?"

Yang Chu answered: "If they do so, their object is to become rich."

Meng: "And when they have become rich, why do they not stop?"

Yang Chu said: "They aim at getting honors."

Meng: "Why then do they not stop when they have got them?"

Yang Chu: "On account of their death."

Meng: "But what can they desire still after their death?"

Yang Chu: "They think of their posterity."

Meng: "But how can their fame be available to their posterity?"

Yang Chu: "For fame's sake they endure all kinds of bodily hardship and mental pain. They dispose of their glory for the benefit of their clan, and even their fellow-citizens profit by it. How much more so do their descendants! Howbeit it becomes those desirous of real fame to be disinterested, and disinterestedness means poverty; and likewise they must be unostentatious, and this is equivalent to humble condition."

How then can fame be disregarded, and how can fame come of itself?

The ignorant, while seeking to maintain fame, sacrifice reality. By doing so, they will have to regret that nothing can rescue them from danger and death, and not only learn the difference between ease and pleasure and sorrow and grief.

If anybody has real greatness, he is poor; if his greatness is spurious, he is rich.

The really good man is not famous; if he be famous, he is not really a good man, for all fame is nothing but falsehood.

One hundred years is the limit of a long life. Not one in a thousand ever attains to it. Yet if they do, still unconscious infancy and old age take up about half this time.

What then is the object of human life? What makes it pleasant? Comfort and elegance, music and beauty. Yet one cannot always gratify the desire for comfort and elegance, nor incessantly enjoy beauty and music.

Besides being warned and exhorted by punishments and rewards, urged forward and repelled by fame and laws, men are constantly rendered anxious. Striving for one vain hour of glory, and providing for the splendor which is to survive their death, they go their solitary ways, analyzing what they hear with their ears and see with their eyes, and carefully considering what is good for body and mind; so they lose the happiest moments of the present, and cannot really give way to these feelings for one hour.

If you pay no regard to life or death, and let them be as they are, how can you be anxious lest your life should end too soon?

Every trace of intelligent and stupid men, of the beautiful and ugly, successful and unsuccessful, right and wrong, is effaced. And whether quickly or slowly is the only point of difference.

If any one cares for one hour's blame or praise so much that, by torturing his spirit and body, he struggles for a name lasting some hundred years after his death, can the halo of glory revive his dried bones, or give him back the joy of living?

If there were a body born complete, I could not possess it, and I could not possess things not to be parted with. For possessing a body or things would be unlawfully appropriating a body belonging to the whole universe and appropriating things belonging to the universe, which no Sage would do.

He who regards as common property a body appertaining to the universe and the things of the universe is a perfect man.

And that is the highest degree of perfection.

THE FOUR CHIMERAS

There are four things which do not allow people to rest: Long Life; Reputation; Rank; Riches.

Those who have them, fear ghosts, fear men, power, and punishment. They are always fugitives. Whether they are killed or live, they regulate their lives by externals.

Those who do not set their destiny at defiance, do not desire a long life; and those who are not too fond of honor, do not desire reputation.

Those who do not want power, desire no rank.

Those who are not avaricious, have no desire for riches.

KANG-HSI'S SACRED EDICT

In every affair retire a step, and you have an advantage.

Seeing men in haste, do not seek to overtake them.

Each grass blade has its drop of dew. The wild birds lay up no stores; but Heaven and Earth are wide. Strange, indeed, if you cannot rest in the duties of your sphere.

If you reject the iron, you will never make the steel.

To starve is a small matter, to lose one's virtue is a great one.

Covet not an empty name.

The modest gain, the self-satisfied lose

The more unlikely I am to be successful, the more diligently will I study.

What have I to do with fate?

Teach children that in friendship one should be one, and two, two; there must be no deception.

Let the root be good, and the fruit shall not be evil.

Culture in manners will make the blustering soldier view the Shi and Shu as his coat of mail.

Becoming manners shall bring back the lovely unity of ancient virtues.

Do you think that, by bearing with insulting persons, I shall fall into dishonor?

Should right principles be separated from right manners, they would no longer be right principles. But without sincerity manners are mere apish bowing and scraping.

Those who say conscience may be good enough, but it does not supply one with food, are fit materials for the cord and the bamboo.

Set not others at variance. Suppress slanders, and protect the innocent. Frame not indictments to defraud and oppress.

Maintain a love of harmony, that throughout your families the common speech shall be, "Let us help one another." Then shall the world be at peace.

Let young and old be as one body, their joys and sorrows as of one family.

Let the instructed lead the way by example. Let the unity of the empire extend to myriad countries, and spread harmony through the world.

Though at the height of fame, you ought in the watches of the night to lay your hand on your breast and ask yourself, "Have I cause o£ shame or not?"

KUAN-YI-WU. 500 B.C. – ON LIFE

Allow the ear to hear what it likes, the eye to see what it likes, the mouth to say what it likes, the body to enjoy the comforts it likes to have, and the mind to do what it likes.

Now, what the ear likes to hear is music, and the prohibition of it is what I call obstruction to the ear.

What the eye likes to look at is beauty, and its not being permitted to regard this beauty I call obstruction of sight.

What the nose likes to smell is perfume, and its not being permitted to smell I call obstruction to scent.

What the mouth likes to talk about is right and wrong; and if it is not permitted to speak, I call it obstruction of the understanding.

The comforts the body enjoys to have are rich food and fine clothing, and if it is not permitted, then I call that obstruction of the senses of the body.

What the mind likes is to be at peace; and its not being permitted rest I call obstruction of the mind's nature.

All these obstructions are a source of the most painful vexation.

YU TSE. 1250 B.C. – ON FAME

He who renounces fame has no sorrow.

Fame is the follower of reality. Now, however, as people pursue fame with such frenzy, does it not really come of itself if it is disregarded? At present fame means honor and regard. Lack of fame brings humbleness and disgrace. Again, ease and pleasure follow upon honor and regard. Sorrow and grief are contrary to human nature; ease and pleasure are in accord with it. These things have reality.

TSE-CHAN. 550 B.C.

SUBLIMITY OF RIGHTEOUSNESS

That in which man is superior to beasts and birds is his mental faculties. Through them he gets righteousness and propriety, and so glory and rank fall to his share. You are only moved by what excites your sense, and indulge only in licentious desires, endangering your lives and natures.

Hear my words. Repent in the morning, and in the evening you will have already gained the wage that will support you.

THE POETRY OF THE CHINESE

SSU-K'UNG T'U, A.D. 834-908

Freighted with eternal principles
Athwart the night's void,
Where cloud masses darken,
And the wind blows ceaselessly around,

Beyond the range of conceptions
Let us gain the center.
And there hold fast without violence,
Fed from an inexhaustible supply.

Like a water-wheel awhirl,
Like the rolling of a pearl;
Yet these but illustrate,
To fools, the final state.

The earth's great axis spinning on,
The never-resting pole of sky —
Let us resolve their Whence and Why,
And blend with all things into One;

Beyond the bounds of thought and dream,
Circling the vasty void as spheres
Those orbits round a thousand years:
Behold the Key that fits my theme.

Rank and wealth within the mind abide,

Then gilded dust is all your yellow gold.
Kings in their fretted palaces grow old;
Youth dwells forever at Contentment's side.
A mist cloud hanging at the river's brim,
Pink almond flowers along the purple bough,
A hut rose-girdled under moon-swept skies,
A painted bridge half-seen in shadows dim,—
These are the splendors of the poor, and thou,
O wine of spring, the vintage of the wise.

CH'ANG CH'IEN. A.D. 720

I sat upon the mountainside and watched.
A tiny barque that skimmed across the lake,
Drifting, like human destiny upon
A world of hidden peril; then she sailed
From out my ken, and mingled with the blue
Of skies unfathomed, while the great round sun
Weakened towards the waves.

TS'EN-TS'AN. A.D. 750

Night is at hand; the night winds fret afar,
The north winds moan. The waterfowl are gone
To cover o'er the sand dunes; dawn alone
Shall call them from the sedges. Some bright star

Mirrors her charms upon the silver shoal;
And I have ta'en the lute, my only friend;
The vibrant chords beneath my fingers blend;
They sob awhile, then as they slip control,

Immortal memories awake, and the dead years

Through deathless voices answer to my strings,
Till from the brink of time's untarnished springs
The melting night recalls me with her tears.

PO CHU-I. A.D. 772

MYSELF

What of myself?
I am like unto the sere chrysanthemum
That is shorn by the frost-blade and, torn from its roots,
Whirled away on the wind.
Once in the valleys of Ch'in and Yung I rambled at will;
Now ring me round the unfriendly plains of the wild folk of Pa.
Oh, galloping dawns with Youth and Ambition riding knee to knee!
Ride on, Youth, with the galloping dawns and dappled days!
I am unhorsed, out-ventured —
I, who crouch by the crumbling embers, old, and gray, and alone.
One great hour of noon with the sky-faring Rukh
I clanged on the golden dome of heaven.
Now in the long dusk of adversity
I have found my palace of contentment, my dream pavilion,
Even the tiny twig of the little humble wren.

LAO TZU

Who knows how white attracts,
Yet always keeps himself within black's shade,
The pattern of humility displayed,
Displayed in view of all beneath the sky,
He in the unchanging excellence arrayed,
Endless return to man's first estate has made.

Who knows how glory shines,
Yet loves disgrace, nor e'er for it is pale;
Behold his presence in a spacious vale,
To which men come from all beneath the sky.
The unchanging excellence completes its tale;
The simple infant man in him we hail.

OU-YANG HSIU. A.D. 1007

In flowing crowds
The moon-born clouds
Cast their light shade
O'er stairs of jade;
And all the moonlit ways are one,
Shining in silver unison.
Yet who can read aright
The mystery of night?

ANON.

Men pass their lives apart like stars that move, but never meet. This eye, how blest it is that the same lamp gives light to both of us! Brief is youth's day. Our temples already tell of waning life. Already half of those we know are spirits; I am moved in the depths of my soul.

ANON

Mother of pity, hear my prayer
That in the endless round of birth
No more may break my heart on earth,
Nor by the windless waters of the Blest
Weary of rest;
That drifting, drifting, I abide not anywhere.
Yet if by Karma's law I must
Resume this mantle of the dust,
Grant me, I pray,
One dewdrop from thy willow spray,
And in the double lotus keep My hidden heart asleep.

ANON. A.D. 1715

Tis we that wail the hour of birth,
'Tis others weep the hour we die.
If I am sad, 'tis others sing;
Should they lament, I will be feasting.
All flows, all passes, like yon stream;
Like yonder wind-wheel all revolves.
We change the fire grill, changing not the fire;
New lamps or old, what matters it?
'Tis laughable that all men flock in crowds
To worship Buddhas and the Genii;
Austerities mean cramp and weariness,
And genuflections to the rites a headache.
'Tis but a tangle of marsh-lights after all,
We cannot seize the shadow of the wind.
What if the gods made answer to our prayers?
With shouts of laughter I should drive the crowd.

A speck upon your ivory fan
You soon may wipe away;

But stains upon the heart or tongue
Remain, alas, for aye.

The voice of the cricket is heard in the hall,
The leaves of the forest are withered and sere;
My sad spirits droop at those chirruping notes,
So thoughtlessly sounding the knell of the year.
Yet why should we sigh at the change of a date,
When life's flowing on in a full, steady tide?
Come, let us be merry with those that we love;
For pleasure in measure there is no one to chide.

CHIA I. 200 B.C.[1] - CALLED THE POE OF CHINA

In dismal, gloomy, crumbling halls,
Betwixt moss-covered, reeking walls
An exiled poet lay.

On his bed of straw reclining,
Half despairing, half repining,
When, athwart the window sill,
In flew a bird of omen ill,
And seemed inclined to stay.

To my book of occult learning
Suddenly I thought of turning,
All the mystery to know
Of that shameless owl or crow,
That would not go away.

---

[1] From "The Lore of Cathay," by W. A. P. Martin, by courtesy of Fleming H. Revell & Co.

"Wherever such a bird shall enter,
'Tis sure some power above has sent her,"
So said the mystic book, "to show
The human dweller forth must go,"
But WHERE it did not say.

Then anxiously the bird addressing,
And my ignorance confessing,
"Gentle bird, in mercy deign
The will of Fate to me explain. Where is my future way?"

It raised its head as if 'twere seeking
To answer me by simply speaking;
Then folded up its sable wing,
Nor did it utter anything,
But breathed a "Welladay!"

More eloquent than any diction,
That simple sigh produced conviction,
Furnishing to me the key
Of the awful mystery That on my spirit lay.

"Fortune's wheel is ever turning,
To human eye there's no discerning
Weal or woe in any state;
Wisdom is to bide your fate."
That is what it seemed to say
By that simple "Welladay."

SU WU

Twin trees whose boughs together twine,

Two birds that guard one nest,
We'll soon be far asunder torn,
As sunrise from the west.

Hearts knit in childhood's innocence,
Long bound in Hymen's ties,
One goes to distant battlefields,
One sits at home and sighs.

Like carrier dove, though seas divide,
I'll seek my lonely mate;
But if afar I find a grave,
You'll mourn my hapless fate.

To us the future's all unknown;
In memory seek relief.
Come, touch the chords you know so well,
And let them soothe our grief.

PAN CHIH YU. 18 B.C. - THE SAPPHO OF CHINA

Of fresh, new silk, all snowy white,
And round as harvest moon,
A pledge of purity and love,
A small but welcome boon.

While summer lasts, borne in the hand,
Or folded on the breast,
'Twill gently soothe thy burning brow,
And charm thee to thy rest.

But, ah! When autumn frosts descend

And winter's winds blow cold,
No longer sought, no longer loved,
'Twill lie in dust and mold.

This silken fan, then, deign accept,
Sad emblem of my lot,
Caressed and fondled for an hour,
Then speedily forgot.

ANON.

Are there not beans in yon boiling pot,
And bean stalks are burning below?
Now why, when they spring from one parent root,
Should they scorch each other so?

LI PO - THE POPE OF HIS AGE

ON DRINKING ALONE BY MOONLIGHT

Here are flowers and here is wine,
But there's no friend with me to join
Hand to hand and heart to heart,
In one full bowl before we part.

Rather, then, than drink alone,
I'll make bold to ask the moon
To condescend to lend her face,
The moment and the scene to grace.

Lo! she answers and she brings
My shadow on her silver wings;
That makes three, and we shall be,

I ween, a merry company.

The modest moon declines the cup,
My shadow promptly takes it up;
And when I dance, my shadow fleet
Keeps measure with my twinkling feet.

Although the moon declines to tipple,
She dances in yon shining ripple;
And when 1 sing, my festive song
The echoes of the moon prolong.

Say, when shall we next meet together?
Surely not in cloudy weather;
For you, my boon companions dear,
Come only when the sky is clear.

PROVERBS AND MAXIMS

ABSENT-MINDEDNESS

Felling a tree to catch the blackbird.
Asking a blind man the road.
Dragging the lake for the moon in the water.
Adding fuel to put out the fire.

ACCURACY

Deviate an inch, lose a thousand miles.

BUSINESS

Better go than send.
Surety for the bow, surety for the arrow.
Great profits, great risks.
Before buying, calculate the selling.
Easy to open a shop; hard to keep it open.
Without a smiling face do not become a merchant.

COMPENSATIONS

The beautiful bird gets caged.

DIFFICULTIES

Easier said than done.
Out of the wolf's den into the tiger's mouth.

DIVINE PROVIDENCE

Man without divine assistance
Cannot move an inch of distance.

EDUCATION

Easy to learn, hard to master.

Husbandry and letters are the two chief professions.

All pursuits are mean in comparison with learning.

Who teaches me for a day is my father for a lifetime.

Scholars are their country's treasure and the richest ornaments of the feast.

Extensive reading is a priceless treasure.

FAMILY

In a united family happiness springs up of itself.

GAMBLING

Losing comes of winning money. Believe in money, sell your house.

FRIENDSHIP

Tigers and deer do not stroll together.

GOVERNMENT

Heaven sees as the people see;

Heaven hears as the people hear.

The guilty emperor exhausts the mandate of Heaven (MENCIUS).

Killing a bad monarch is no murder (MENCIUS).

Would you know politics, read history.

The emperor is the father of his people, not a master to be served by slaves.

GRATITUDE

Lambs have the grace to suck kneeling.

HEEDLESSNESS

In at one ear, out at the other.

Man cannot reach perfection in a hundred years;
He can fall in a day with time to spare.

HONESTY

Just scales and full measure injure no man.

Never do what you wouldn't have known.

However much you promise, never fail to pay,
or
Do not vary your promise for any price.

HUMANITY

Kindness is greater than law. Guide the blind over the bridge.

HUSBANDS AND WIVES

If they match by nature, marry them.
Every family has a Goddess of Mercy.

Naught must divide the married pair;
Its weight the steelyard cannot spare!

Who is the wife of one, cannot eat the rice of two.
In the husband fidelity, in the wife obedience.

HUMILITY

Falling hurts least those who fly low.

INDUSTRY

Those who will not work shall not eat.

INSTINCT

Plants surpass men in recognizing spring.
Does the swallow know the wild goose's course?

KNOWLEDGE

Schools hide future premiers.
The pen conveys one's meaning a thousand miles.

LAWSUITS

Win your lawsuit, lose your money.
If one family has a lawsuit, ten families are involved.

VANITY OF LIFE

Naked we came, naked we go.
The Great Wall stands; the builder is gone.

MAN

Mind is lord of man.
Virtuous men are a king's treasure.

OPPORTUNITY

Strike while the iron is hot.
Spilt water cannot be gathered up.

PHYSICIANS

The cleverest doctor cannot save himself.

Easy to get a thousand prescriptions; hard to obtain a cure.

He that takes medicine and neglects diet, wastes the skill of the physician.

Only those become priests who cannot earn a living.

One son becomes a priest, nine generations are sure of Heaven.

PROCRASTINATION

Never waste time.
Procrastination is the thief of time.

PRACTICAL RELIGION

God loves all men.

Better do a kindness near home than go far to burn incense.

To save one life is better than to build a seven-story pagoda.

SELF-CONTROL

Think twice — and say nothing.

YOUTH

In the boy see the man.
The mark must be made in youth.

WINE

Leisure breeds lust.
Wine is the discoverer of secrets.
Intoxication is not the wine's fault, but the man's.

WOMAN

The good-looking woman needs no paint.

Never quarrel with a woman.

Three tenths of good looks are due to nature; seven tenths to dress.

SERVICE

Injure others, injure yourself.

One generation plants the trees; another sits in their shade.

SKILL

Unskilled fools quarrel with their tools.

Better Master of one than Jack of all trades.

VIRTUE

Better die than turn your back on reason.

Look not on temptation, and your mind will be at rest.

It is a little thing to starve to death; it is a serious matter to lose one's virtue.

GENERAL

When men come face to face, their differences vanish.

Do not neglect your own in order to weed another's field.

Time flies like an arrow, days and months like a shuttle.

MORAL MAXIMS

The man of first-rate excellence is virtuous independently of instruction; he of the middling class is so after instruction; the lowest order of men are vicious in spite of instruction.

In the days of affluence always think of poverty; do not let want come upon you and make you remember with sorrow the days of plenty.

Without the wisdom of the learned, the clown could not be governed; without the labor of the clown, the learned could not be fed.

The cure of ignorance is study, as meat is that of hunger.

The mind is its own place, and in itself Can make a heaven of Hell, a hell of Heaven.

The same tree may produce sour and sweet fruit; the same mother may have a virtuous and vicious progeny.

It is equally criminal in the governor and the governed to violate the laws.

As the scream of the eagle is heard when she has passed over, so a man's name remains after his death.

Questions of right and wrong (with reference to right and wrong) are every day arising; if not listened to, they die away of themselves.

If the domestic duties be duly performed, where is the necessity of going afar to burn incense?

Doubt and distraction are on earth; the brightness of truth in Heaven.

Meeting with difficulties, we think of our relations; on the brink of danger we rely on our friends.

Among mortals who is faultless?

Do not love idleness and hate labor; do not be diligent in the beginning and in the end lazy.

If there be no faith in our words, of what use are they?

If riches can be acquired with propriety, then acquire them; but let not unjust wealth be sought for with violence.

Wine and good dinners make abundance of friends, but in the time of adversity not one is to be found.

Let every man sweep the snow from before his own doors and not trouble himself about the frost on his neighbor's tiles.

Though a tree be a thousand chang in height, its leaves must fall down and return to its root.

Worldly reputation and pleasure are destructive to virtue; anxious thoughts are injurious to the body.

Better be upright with poverty than depraved abundance.

He whose virtue exceeds his talents is a good man; he whose talents exceed his virtue is a mean one.

In a field of melons do not pull up your shoe; under a plum tree do not adjust your cap (be very careful of your actions under circumstances of suspicion).

The man of worth is really great without being proud; the mean man is proud without being really great.

It is said in the Ye-King that "of those men whose talent is inconsiderable, while their station is eminent, and of those whose knowledge is small, while their schemes are large, there are few who do not become miserable."

Though a man may be utterly stupid, he is very perspicacious when reprehending the bad actions of others;

though he may be very intelligent, he is dull enough while excusing his own faults; do you only correct yourselves on the same principle that you correct others, and excuse others on the same principle that you excuse yourselves.

The artful are loquacious, the simple are silent; the artful toil, the simple enjoy ease; the artful are rogues, the simple virtuous; the artful are miserable, the simple happy. Oh, that all in the empire were artful and simple! Punishments would then be abolished. Superiors would enjoy tranquillity, and inferiors would be obedient. The manners would be pure, and vile actions become extinct.

Do not anxiously hope for what is not yet come; do not vainly regret what is already past.

If your schemes do not succeed, of what use is it to regret their failure? If they do not flourish, what is the use of noisy complaints? When a heart, devoted to gain, is intent on any object, then virtue is set aside; where interested views exist, there a regard for the public welfare is extinguished.

Men's passions are like water: when water has once flowed over, it cannot be restored; when the passions have once been indulged, they cannot be restrained. Water must be kept in by dikes; the passions must be ruled by the laws of propriety.

Low courage is the resentment of the blood and spirits; noble courage is the resentment of propriety and justice. The former of these.no man should possess; the latter no man should be without.

Without ascending the mountain, we cannot judge of the height of heaven; without descending into the valley, we cannot judge of the depth of the earth; without listening to the maxims left by the ancient kings, we cannot know the excellence of learning.

In making a candle we seek for light, in reading a book we seek for reason; light to illuminate a dark chamber, reason to enlighten a man's heart.

If you have fields and will not plow them, your barns will be empty; if you have books and will not give instruction, your offspring will be ignorant; if your barns be empty, your years and months will be unsupplied; if your offspring be ignorant, propriety and justice will not abound among them.

Though an affair may be easily accomplished, if it be not attended to, it will never be completed; though your son be well-disposed, if he be not instructed, he will still remain ignorant.

If you love your son, give him plenty of the cudgel; if you hate your son, cram him with dainties.

The small birds look around them and eat; the swallow goes to sleep without apprehension. He who possesses an enlarged and sedate mind, will have great happiness; but the man whose schemes are deep, will have great depth of misery.

When the mirror is highly polished, the dust will not defile it; when the heart is enlightened with wisdom, licentious vices will not arise in it.

The fishes, though deep in the water, may be hooked; the birds, though high in the air, may be shot; but man's heart only is out of our reach. The heavens may be measured, the earth may be surveyed; the heart of man alone is not to be known. In painting the tiger, you may. delineate his skin, but not his bones; in your acquaintance with a man you may know his face, but not his heart. You may sit opposite to, and converse with him, while his mind is hidden from you as by a thousand mountains.

Forming resentments with mankind may be called "planting misery"; putting aside virtuous deeds, instead of practicing them, may be called "robbing oneself."

When a man of a naturally good propensity has much wealth, it injures his acquisition of knowledge; when a worthless man has much wealth, it increases his faults.

In enacting laws, rigor is indispensable; in executing them, mercy.

Do not consider any vice as trivial, and therefore practice it; do not consider any virtue as unimportant, and therefore neglect it.

If men's desires and wishes be laudable, Heaven will certainly further them.

Those who have discharged their duty as children, will in their turn have dutiful children of their own; the obstinate and untoward will again produce offspring of the same character. To convince you, only observe the rain from the thatched roof, where drop follows drop without the least variation.

He who tells me of my faults is my teacher; he who tells me of my virtues does me harm.

Let your words be few and your companions select; thus you will avoid remorse and repentance, thus you will avoid sorrow and shame.

Be temperate in drinking, and your mind will be calm; restrain your impetuosity, and your fortunes will remain uninjured.

If you wish to know what most engages a man's thoughts, you have only to listen to his conversation (or A man's conversation is the mirror of his thoughts).

In our actions we should accord with the will of Heaven; in our words we should consult the feelings of men.

Throughout life beware of performing acts of animosity; in the whole empire let there not exist a revengeful-minded man. It is very well for you to injure others; but what think you of others returning those injuries on yourself? The tender blade is nipped by the frost; the frost is dissipated by the sun; and worthless man will always suffer rubs from others as bad as themselves.

Knowing what is right, without practicing it, denotes a want of proper resolution.

Poverty and ruin must in the end be proportioned to a man's wickedness and craft; for these are qualities which Heaven will not suffer to prevail. Were riches and honor the proper result of crafty villainy, the better part of the world must fatten on the winds.

The best cure for drunkenness is, whilst sober, to observe a drunken man.

The opening flower blooms alike in all places; the moon sheds an equal radiance on every mountain and every river. Evil exists only in the heart of men; all other things tend to show the benevolence of Heaven towards the human race.

A man without thought for the future must soon have present sorrow.

When you put on your clothes, remember the labor of the weaver; when you eat your daily bread, think of the hardships of the husbandman.

A man is ignorant of his own failings as the- ox is unconscious of his great strength.

The poverty of others is not to be ridiculed, for the decrees of destiny are in the end equal; nor are the infirmities of age a fit subject for laughter, since they must at last be the portion of us all. When the day that is passing over us is gone, our lives are proportionably contracted. What reason, then, have the fish to be merry, when the water in which they swim is ebbing away?

An immoderate use of dainties generally ends in disease, and pleasure, when past, is converted into pain. It is better to avert the malady by care than to have to apply the physic after it has appeared.

Though the white gem be cast into the dirt, its purity cannot be (lastingly) sullied; though the good man live in a vile place, his heart cannot be depraved. As the fir and the cypress withstand the rigors of the winter, so resplendent wisdom is safe in difficulty and danger.

If a man wish to attain to the excellence of superior beings, let him first cultivate the virtues of humanity; for if not perfect in human virtue, how shall he reach immortal perfection?

Man is born without knowledge, and when he has obtained it, very soon becomes old; when his experience is ripe, death suddenly seizes him.

A man's prosperous or declining condition may be gathered from the proportion of his waking to his sleeping hours.

Unsullied poverty is always happy, while impure wealth brings with it many sorrows.

The goodness of a house does not consist in its lofty halls, but in its excluding the weather; the fitness of clothes does not consist in their costliness, but in their make and warmth; the use of food does not consist in its rarity, but in its satisfying the appetite; the excellence of a wife consists not in her beauty, but in her virtue.

The fame of men's good actions seldom goes' beyond their own doors, but their evil deeds are carried to a thousand miles distance.

The sincerity of him who assents to everything, must be small; and he who praises you inordinately to your face, must be altogether false.

If sincerity be wanting between the prince and his minister, the nation will be in disorder; if between father and son, the family will be discordant; if between brothers, their affection will be loosened; if between friends, their intercourse will be distant.

Though powerful medicines be nauseous to the taste, they are good for the disease; though candid advice be unpleasant to the ear, it is profitable to the conduct.

To show compassion towards the people by remitting the severity of the taxes, is the virtue of the prince;

and to offer up their possessions, sinking their private views in regard for the public, is the duty of the people.

Though the life of a man be short of a hundred years, he gives himself as much anxiety as if he were to live a thousand.

If a man does not receive guests at home, he will meet with very few hosts abroad.

Without a clear mirror a woman cannot know the state of her own face; without a true friend a man cannot discern the errors of his own actions.

A man should choose a friend who is better than himself; if only like himself, he had better have none. There are plenty of acquaintances in the world, but very few real friends.

In her accomplishments it is not requisite for a woman to display talent of a famous or uncommon description, in her face it is not requisite that she should be very handsome; her conversation need not be very pointed or eloquent, her work need not be very exquisite or surpassing.

A virtuous woman is a source of honor to her husband; a vicious one causes him disgrace.

A man's patrimony must suffer by trifling and idleness, as it must flourish by diligence. The chief rule to be observed in one's plan of life is to be strenuous in the beginning and to increase one's exertions to the last.

Even the carriers of burdens may, by honesty and diligence, obtain a sufficiency. The proverb says: "Every blade of grass has its share of the dews of heaven"; and "Though the birds of the forest have no garners, the wide world is all before them."

He who wishes to know the road through the mountains must ask those who have already trodden it (i.e., we must look to the experienced for instruction).

It is better to believe that a man possess good qualities than to assert that he does not.

The mischiefs of fire, or water, or robbers, extend only to the body; but those of pernicious doctrines, to the mind.

The original tendency of a man's heart is to do right, and if a due caution be observed, it will not of itself go wrong.

As it is impossible to please men in all things, our only care should be to satisfy our own consciences.

A man's countenance is a sufficient index of his prosperity or adversity, without asking him any questions.

Adversity is necessary to the development of man's virtues.

He who neglects to study diligently in his youth, will, when he is old, repent that he put it off until too late.

He who studies ten years in obscurity, will, when once preferred, be known universally.

It is too late to pull the rein when the horse has gained the brink of the precipice; the time for stopping the leak is past when the vessel is in the midst of the river.

If a stream be not confined, it will soon flow away and become dry; if wealth be not economized, there will be no limits to its expenditure, and it will soon be wasted.

It is easy to convince a wise man, but to reason with a fool is a difficult undertaking.

Speak of men's virtues as if they were your own, and of their vices as if you were liable to their punishment.

Mencius said: "All men concur in despising a glutton, because he gives up everything that is valuable for the sake of pampering what is so contemptible."

What man shall dare to oppose him whose words are consistent with reason, and whose actions are squared by the rule of rectitude?

To the contented, even poverty and obscurity bring happiness, while to the ambitious, wealth and honors are productive of misery.

As the light of a single star tinges the mountains of many regions, so a single unguarded expression injures the virtue of a whole life.

The evidence of a single glance should not be relied on as true, nor are words spoken behind a man's back deserving of much credence.

Though a poor man should live in the midst of a noisy market, no one will ask about him; though a rich man should bury himself among the mountains, his relations will come to him from a distance.

Knowledge is boundless, but the capacity of one man is limited.

Plausible words are not so good as straightforward conduct; a man whose deeds are enlightened by virtue, need not be nice about his expressions.

A single conversation across the table with a wise man is better than ten years' mere study of books.

By a single day's practice of virtue, though happiness may not be attained, yet misery may be kept at a distance; by a single day of ill doing, happiness is prevented.

No medicine can procure long life even to the ministers of the emperor; no money can purchase for any man a virtuous posterity.

A single false move loses the game.

Prudence will carry a man all over the world, but the impetuous find every step difficult.

BIBLIOGRAPHY AND SOURCES

SAMUEL COULING, M.A., The Encyclopaedia Sinica.

Oxford University. Sir J. F. DAVIS, Chinese Moral Maxims. London. 1823.

DE GROOT, The Religious Systems of China. Sir R. K. DOUGLAS, The Literature and Language of China.

H. A. GILES, History of Chinese Literature.

Appleton and Co., New York. Dr. W. A. P. MARTIN, The Lore of Cathay.

Fleming H. Revell and Co., New York. WILLIAM SCARBOROUGH, Chinese Proverbs. London. 1873.

ARTHUR H. SMITH, Proverbs and Common Sayings of the Chinese. 1902.

D. T. SUZUKI, Brief History of Chinese Philosophy. . Probsthain & Co. London. 1914. The Chinese Classics. Translated by Prof. JAMES

LEGGE. Oxford University Press. The Sacred Books of China. Translated by Prof. JAMES LEGGE. Oxford University Press.

LIONEL GILES (Translated by), The Sayings of Lao Tzu. John Murray, London.

L. CRANMER-BYNG (Translated by), The Book of Odes (Shi King). John Murray, London.

LIONEL GILES (Translated by), Taoist Teachings. John Murray, London.

LIONEL GILES (Translated by), Sayings of Confucius. John Murray, London.

LIONEL GILES (Translated by), Musings of a Chinese Mystic. John Murray, London.

These books are in the "Wisdom of the East" Series Imported by E. P. Dutton Co.

www.ingramcontent.com/pod-product-compliance
Lightning Source LLC
Chambersburg PA
CBHW071022180726
48291CB00004B/1584

* 9 7 8 1 9 2 7 0 7 7 1 2 2 *